Healing Feelings Series

Practical Life Skills and Related Research

By Patrice Joy, MA

Illustrated by Kristen Croxton, BA

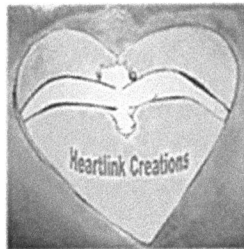

Heartlink Creations

Practical Life Skills and Related Research

ISBN 978-1-7325939-5-4

Library of Congress Control Number: 2018910
Editors: C. J. Wright, Alida Coughlin

Illustrator: Kristen Croxton

Printed in the United States of America
First Printing, 2019

Printed by KDP
Available from Amazon.com, CreateSpace.com, and other retail outlets

Published by Heartlink Creations
Bedford, KY

Inquiries: healingfeelings333@gmail.com

Contents

Acknowledgement

I want to thank my family and friends for the exciting adventures that are incorporated in the Healing Feelings Series. The contents of these were taken from times we shared as they were growing up. The sprinklets and pestlets and puppets were the basis of learning moral values and the power of positive interactions. My family, including five sons Brent, Trevor, Ed, Patrick and Kevin; daughter Lisa; eight grandchildren Tara, Heather, Savannah, Matthew, Cory, Dylan, Elliott, and Abe; and three great granddaughters Ava, Leah and Natalie gave the inspiration for these stories. I am grateful for my four daughters in law, Cindy, Anne, Julie and Shannon and my soul granddaughter, Paige.

Thanks to my 'soul sisters' in the Native Women's Wisdom Circle who have been there for me through thick and thin. My friends Joy, Carol, Carla, Donna, Leslie, Deb and Angela shared love and faith to encourage me. I will always hold Momfeather, Pat, Koon Dog, Amy and Bev most dear in my heart through time.

I offer special thanks to my son Ed and my husband Dan who helped a great deal with the editing and publishing process. I am grateful for the talented illustrators, Kristen and Nancy, who have brought my stories to life in color and form; and for my loyal friends Alida, CJ and the publishers. Without all of you, I couldn't have finished this project.

OpenDyslexic font is more easily read

by persons with some common symptoms of dyslexia.

See full series and other books by Patrice Joy

Healing Feelings Series

Book 1: Meet the Sprinklets & Pestlets

Book 2: The Sprinklets & Pestlets Take Over Earth

Book 3: Teddy the Turtle's Family & Friends

Book 4: Teddy, Bonnie & the Bullies

Book 5: Play Potentials Booklet

Book 6: Practical Life Skills & Related Research

Pet Adventures

Book 1: Buffy Meets Lucky

Book 2: Friends Forever

Dolphins Dreaming

Feather Friends

Self-Awareness Sprinklet & Pestlet Cards

Introduction

This manual is a report on the research in Vibrational Medicine and other mind/body/spirit therapies in the Healing Feelings Series. It includes concepts from Neuro Linguistic Programming (NLP), Self-hypnosis, Cranial Electric Stimulation (CES). Epigenetics in DNA/RNA Behavior, Neuroplasticity, Mindfulness, Reiki, Stress, Immunology, Emotional Intelligence, Relaxation Response Cognitive Behavior Therapy (CBT), Positive Psychology, HeartMath, Emotional Freedom Technique and Collective Unconscious Theories of the Human Potential Movement in Integrative Health.

The 'Parent's Role' section offers suggestions for parents to set up the environment to develop the prerequisites for optimal learning and life success. It gives a procedure to train the respect method of cooperative discipline, creative training and inner directives including these dynamics: self-reliance, self-image, goal setting, chores/rules/rewards, action/reaction, development of maturity and organizational skills and establishing boundaries and bridges.

The teen section is entitled 'Teens in These Troubled Times.' It provides suggestions for youth to handle peer cultural and social pressures. The discovery of one's true identity with gang influence is more challenging in these changing times. Self-questioning is a key to self-awareness. Reaching within is the process implemented to find the optimal path to quality of life.

SECTION ONE

Overview of Mind–Body–Spirit Principals and Related Fields

Chapter One: The Philosophy of Sprinklets and Pestlets

Thoughts are based on attitudes and beliefs. These lead to feelings of the same type. Positive feelings create energy that makes those sharing it feel warm and glowing inside. They are called sprinklets because they make people feel like blessings from the stars are sprinkling all around them. Sprinklets appear as six-pointed twinkling stars that can transform people into feeling safe, calm, joyful and peaceful. This uplifting energy offers benefits mentally, physically, psychologically and spiritually. When loving kindness directs the person's choices, virtues of respect and integrity are the resulting behavior.

Pestlets are pesky thoughts and feelings that block your good, so they are cube shaped. These harmful thoughts and feelings come from destructive attitudes which freeze and block emotions leaving people with a cold feeling. They bring harmful energy that gets in the way of receiving the positive energy of sprinklets.

If a person lives in denial of these repetitive pesky patterns, they become boxed in by hurtful relations. Their communication and ability to form new meaningful contact is hindered and their level of joy is reduced by negativity. A dark gloomy existence dominates the moods of people who are absorbed with these pestlet energies. The thoughts that cycle the brain in these emotional states create biochemical changes mentally and physically that are detrimental to the well-being.

If people bury pestlet energy inside themselves, their self-understanding and empathy for others becomes blocked. When feelings are not released in a constructive manner, the wounded ego dominates the personality. This becomes a key factor in the dishonest games people play to bury and soothe this distortion of self-worth. Psychological trauma from emotional, verbal, or physical abuse can create an overextended ego that needs constant attention and power gratification. Everyone either enjoys or suffers the outcome of their choices by bringing in blessings or problems.

Psychology of Puppetry

The puppet plays in the Loving Kindness Creative Learning Kit are based on themes of special holidays. The intent is to connect families with community sharing and to find a deeper understanding of the quality of life. The seasonal puppet plays were written to help explain the true meaning of each special occasion. They help a person reconnect to the positive values in the roots of society and our family heritage. The story lessons reach within the feeling level to bring better awareness of ourselves and our effect on others.

When the mind is free from the cycle of endless games that protects the wounded ego, the self-concept improves, and the individual can become light-hearted and joyful. As a person learns to love and accept ones' self, he or she can love unconditionally. Then the "Happy Inner Child" is born again in those of all ages.

The stories are presented in the format of short puppet plays to be acted by students, teachers, counselors, family and friends. Awareness Activities are included at the end of each puppet play. These are designed to facilitate a deeper awareness of one's feelings, motivation and the responsibility that we each have to one another. behavioral games and crafts are provided to heighten the fun.

As the child portrays the puppet, he or she can more completely understand their own thoughts, feelings and actions. By mirroring themselves through the puppet, greater understanding and responsibility for their repercussions can take place. They provide a tool for problem solving techniques. The child can discover at an emotional level what the puppet does to work out positive solutions to everyday situations. Birthdays and special occasions can be celebrated for adults and children in puppet plays. Holiday Puppet shows were written to help explain the true meaning of events for each special season. Involvement of the puppet parties teaches how to take the joy of the holiday into everyday life.

The Theory of Vibrational Therapies

This is a vibrationally based Universe. Everything vibrates and the 'Law of Attraction' sorts out matching vibrational frequencies. All emotions hold a vibration. Peaceful and joyful energy is supportive to optimal thinking and better health. Emotions of anger, fear and guilt drain energy and destroy health of mind, body and spirit. Our feelings tell us what vibrational frequency we are tuned to. They return to you precisely what you are putting out. Our words attract what we can expect. What you say is what you get in this vibrational attraction theory. It is critically important to visualize what you do want, instead of what you don't want. The mind acts as a force field drawing to it what is expressed within. Thoughts create a composite of vibration.

The concept of Vibrational Therapy is based on the energy that is emitted from all living things. Through the process of one's output of thoughts and resulting feelings, sound waves are emitted. The individual acts as a magnetic receiving station to draw in higher or lower energies depending on output of the person. We are all using these natural laws to create fulfilment of goals.

When those involved are in conflict, the vibration takes on a density and broadcasts a chaotic frequency. When these dense, concentrated energy fields are replaced with uplifting energy, harmony in these fields can bring improved health. Healing can then be activated by raising the vibration of a cell, organ, gland and thought pattern. Quantum Physics has discovered that by raising our energy or vibrational level, we are enhancing light, adding energy to the fields in and around our bodies, and balancing our emotions. This aids in creating and restoring wellness and equilibrium.

Treatment with vibration has been practiced by ancient civilizations throughout time. This is a return to the wisdom of natural laws from indigenous cultures in Africa, Australia, China, Japan, India and Asia, who used the vibration of color, sound and stones as means to bring inner balance. Monks throughout Europe, Tibet, Peru and other countries were masters at visualization and chanted hours as they prayed and did daily chores. They discovered they had greater health in all aspects of their life and relationships by implementing these practices.

Vibrational Therapy may be rapidly becoming a science of the future in the medical field. Several modalities access the Chi Life Force (primary life energy) such as Holy Fire Reiki, Chi-Lel Qigong, Mudras, Asanas and Yoga. Energetic Touch, Potent Point, Acupuncture, Cranial Electrical Stimulation (CES), Heart Math, Emotional Freedom Technique and Axitonal Therapy open the flow of energy in the body meridians which are lines of energy discovered in ancient eastern medicine.

Indigenous medicine persons throughout many cultures have extraordinary knowledge about harmonics as a key for transformation. Sound waves bridge different dimensional zones in altered states. Vibrations are coming to us now from the fifth to the ninth dimensions and beyond. Each color and tone have a different vibratory effect on living tissue and cells.

The Vibrational Benefits of Color

Several cultures believe in the healing power of the color spectrum. The reflection of color through prisms and glass was used in ancient Egypt as a treatment for ailments. Wearing specific colors according to a disorder was also recommended. In Chinese medicine each organ is associated with a color. The practice of qigong links healing sounds with color. Ayurvedic medicine in India dates back thousands of years. It connects the elements and the energy of color to restore harmony. American Indians relate to the colorful life force in nature.

When color enters the eye, it travels thru the electrical nervous system and is directed to the area of the body that recognizes that frequency of color. This causes cellular and hormonal changes to occur thus bringing the body into synchronization. Color imagery can take a person into the unconscious, or nonverbal state and elicit memories. Color serves to support one's vital life force. This process can influence our emotions and overall health by supplying the frequency we need to keep our mind and body in balance.

Since color and sound have vibration, these can both be added to an image to get even greater impact. For example, the frequency of light is measured in trillions of cycles per second and sound at ten thousand cycles per second. When the mind is focused on the vibration of a specific color, multi-dimensional effects are created. Each color's vibration is associated with different qualities. The vibratory frequency of every color aides the benefit of positive energy and demonstrates the destructive effects of negativity. The color of each sprinklet and pestlet represent their specific energetic properties.

For example, Kindness Sprinklet is peach. This is a combination of the color tones of red, orange and yellow which is representative of maternal nurturing and fraternal protection. Loving Sprinklet is green and pink. When a person chooses to demonstrate love, virtues of respect and integrity are the resulting behavior. These two colors hold the vibration of the heart to facilitate the flow of loving energy. A lack of self-love causes a lack of kind self-care.

The energy of Joyful Sprinklet is so vibrant it explodes like yellow sunbeams. Joy is the frequency of bliss and magical delight that comes from connecting with nature. The energy of peace can also be found in nature. Peaceful sprinklet is blue representing the color of inner calm, tranquility and serenity. The shade of blue is in peaceful skies filled with fluffy clouds and in still water and gentle flowing streams.

Hopeful Sprinklet is represented by all the colors of the rainbow. This holds the potential of better things to come. Thoughts act like a magnetic force attracting blessings for which we are thankful. Gratitude is based on the concept that what we think about, we bring about. Lavender is the color of Grateful Sprinklet which brings transformation of the things we hope will come into being.

Being honest with oneself demonstrates standing by your words and being grounded. Brown is the color of Honesty Sprinklet which represents a connection to Earth energy. Dishonesty creates a separation within. There is a lack of self-awareness and communication with others. The color of Dishonesty Pestlet is a lime green.

Angry Pestlet is based in the lack of honesty which creates self-denial. Until a person looks at themselves with honesty, they cannot correct imbalances in their personality. Red is representative of the anger vibration. Raging Pestlet is the demonstration of accelerated, obsessive anger and is represented by the color of blazing red. Depression Pestlet is often buried anger. Its pinkish-red color represents hiding anger behind love. It is in the category of the harmful effects of pestlets caused by harboring anger at past or present events.

Brownish red is the color that depicts the frequency of Smug Pestlet. The energy of a smug person is characterized by anger and insecurity. Low self-esteem causes these individuals to act bigger than others. There is a dominating aspect of bully behavior in those with a damaged self-concept who need to prove their power and worth.

If guilt from past behavior or choices is present, the good may be blocked due to judgement and self-persecution. Guilty Pestlet is characterized by brownish green and relates to these self-destructive patterns. This fosters a sense of being undeserving of opportunities with a need to suffer and struggle. Success in relationships and financial gain are consequently limited. Internal judgement and negativity affect the person's future life choices. It is important to have recognition of ones' actions and a willingness to change. Dwelling on the self-persecution of guilt causes the person to prevent good outcomes. This can lead to a tendency of isolation and inability to have socialization.

Sadness, loneliness and grieving are aspects of feeling blue. Victim and pity patterns can result in blue colored Sadness Pestlet. The tones of navy and darker purplish blue relate to feelings of isolation in Loneliness Pestlet. It is extremely important to have a time to process loss and have closure. Yet, long-term grief is damaging and impedes moving on in life. It is represented by the bluish grey color of stagnation in Grieving Pestlet.

Worry is also the frequency of grey and represents a void of faith. Worry creates inner turmoil, which involves little forward motion. Many times, the lack of action and risk taking is caused by fear. This relates to the spectrum of colors in the grey and black tones of Fearful Pestlet and Worry Pestlet. A dark gloomy existence dominates the moods of those absorbed with these energies.

Color Therapy, or Chromatherapy is based on the premise that certain colors have restorative properties. Their vibration enhances the absorption of color from light. This supplies what a person may be lacking to keep their body and mind balanced. Color meditation involves visualizing specific colors to attract the vibrational properties from the color of focus. Color breathing is another form of meditation which involves focusing on specific colors in coordination with breathing routines.

Individuals using Color Therapy have reported:

Improved health	Stabilized moods	Better Memory
Greater alertness	Increased vitality	Calm Inner peace
Improved complexion and skin tone	Happier	Light-hearted

Healing Properties of Color Vibration

* Red motivates action. It is a strong vibration and can be associated with anger, rage and love.
* Orange aides in pain relief, nurturing, creativity and building self-esteem.
* Yellow is the color of new beginnings, fulfillment of our dreams and child-like joy.
* Green is the color of healing and regeneration. It is associated with the heart.
* Pink represents unconditional love; it stimulates purity of intent and awakens truth.
* Blue is the color of peace; it is the symbol of spiritual understanding of one's purpose.
* Shades of darker blue can relate to sadness and separation.
* Shades of violet and purple are the colors of transmutation, releasing and clearing.
* Brown is associated with grounding and steadfastness.
* White has the spectrum of all the colors of the rainbow. It is excellent for overall healing and amplifies the specific benefits of each color. It is the symbol of purity and power and hope.
* Black is associated with fear. Yet, it can be used to help us find the light within the dark.
* When a person remains centered in the positive energetics, a force field is created to bring alignment with the highest outcome and success in life endeavors. The co-creative power is up to the individual to make wise choices and establish a life filled with joyous adventures.

Chapter Two: Scientific Research in Related Fields

Scientists are proving the power of the mind to control the body. The practice of *Mindfulness* with a focus on sensory awareness and breathing can cause physical changes in the brain to protect our immune system. Mindful Meditation is a form of controlled contemplation on a single image or peaceful scene formulated by John Kabbot Zin. This replaces the endless stream of thoughts and head noise. When a person can control the endless chatter of mental overload, it is then possible to tune into the present surroundings and input.

In addition to being more attentive and finding enhanced quality of life, neuroscientists found the patients in these studies had fewer age-related changes. Gray matter that comes with aging was reduced in a part of the brain that helps control motor skills and learning ability. Their patients in the study were also less sensitive to pain, with emotional benefits of less anxiety and depression.

Daniel G. Amen, M.D is a pioneer in the field of Neuroplasticity. This is based on the theory that what we focus our minds on reshapes and rewires the brain in crucial ways. It builds the autoimmune system and protects the cells from inflammatory conditions. The mind is the co-creator in a person's experiences and affects the biochemical balance of their hormones and quality of health. In his book "Magnificent Mind at Any Age", Dr. Amen explains ways to unleash your brain's maximum potential. The world-renown Amen Clinic has shown progress treating anxiety, depression, memory problems, ADD and insomnia.

Scientific research in the placebo effect and the power of belief are proving people are magnetic force fields. In Epigenetics, the cellular behavior of DNA has been shown to be affected by thoughts, moods, diet, exercise and stress levels. Behavioral psychology supports the power of positive thinking to lower signs of aging and symptoms of illness.

The Power of the Mind

The mind acts like a computer and can't tell the difference between imagining every detail of a fearful event and one that has really happened. Some people think of the worst possible outcome and dwelled on it until it makes them a nervous wreck. These people are taking their stress levels and destructive reactionary body biochemistry through a false sense of reality by the focus of thoughts and resulting negative emotions. Their mind becomes tied up with problems and the inspiration of solutions is blocked. The mind is locked into repeated, racing patterns of 'go-mode.' Instead of experiencing and projecting this frantic mental pattern, be a constructive role-model. Think in beneficial ways.

Parent yourself in healthy ways. Each person has been affected by the supportive nurturing and by earlier harm or neglect. Thought replacement principals are at the foundation of the process to balance parenting tapes. Use this mind-in-action-principal to create a new habit of harmonious thoughts:

Take a deep breath through the nose and inhale a thought of gratitude for a peaceful resolution to the situation; then exhaled the worrisome thought.

In addition to psychologically dealing with the mind and emotional functions, physical factors must also be addressed. A diet change affects the ability to focus the mind. Regulate sugar and caffeine intake to calm the nerves. Enjoy Chamomile herb tea instead of other caffeine stimulating coffee and tea. Calming the nervous system, taking control over reactions and stopping the habit of focusing on negatives and repressed fear fosters optimum brain function. This provides a calmer composure and more positive outlook.

You can then start functioning from an internal focus of hopeful alternatives, allowing the flow of creativity. The ability to control reactions to the outside world and to internal fears provides growth emotionally, mentally and physically. People are always thinking and believing something that either drains or builds energy. A person's thoughts are always creative, whether they consciously know it or not.

Through this process, they are setting action in motion. To the degree a person sees harmony instead of discord, she/he will demonstrate these life events and relationships. Begin to make choices to use this creative power for benefit. The first step is to observe oneself, using objective mindfulness to pay attention to thought patterns. With this active awareness replaced worry with a thought of a hopeful outcome. Then practice a relaxation technique to breathe away the problem.

Self-Hypnosis for Whole Brain Activation

All effective hypnosis is self-hypnosis. By your choice, you are simply accepting thoughts directed by a hypnotist. You can stop these suggestions to your unconscious mind by declaring they are invalid. If you are with a hypno-therapist, you are repeating what the therapist suggests and allowing your mind to be directed. Hypnotherapy can be used effectively to filter destructive thought obsessions.

Mind is the initiator and each person is a co-creator of your life experience. It is important to visualize what you do want instead of what you don't want. By changing your thoughts, you are changing your brain wave frequency. Your thoughts are a doorway into these realities in your unconscious mind.

Thoughts create a "thought form" which is a composite of vibrations. Implement the 'gratitude-thought' of the desired goal that has already been fulfilled. Become actively aware of harmony, rather than discord. Then body systems will calm down. Health, mental function, emotional stability and energy levels will improve accordingly. Thoughts create energy waves.

High Beta waves are measured as a jagged line of extreme stress and crisis. **Beta** is the level of regular conversation. **Alpha** brain waves look like a gentle flow on the brain wave charts. This lower frequency creates relaxation and is where creativity and memory take place. **Theta** is an even lower brain wave level that goes deep into the unconscious mind. It could be related to anesthesia during surgery and is where old emotional wounds are stored. PTSD and repressed traumas are accessed in this brain wave frequency. In **Delta** you are connected to everything as vibration. Delta brain waves are akin to a comatose state.

Affirmations are a form of controlled thoughts. For an affirmation to work, there must be an agreement between the conscious and unconscious mind. Self-hypnosis acts as a bridge between these two parts of your mind to reveal any incongruences. Buried guilt can halt manifestation of success in affirming your intention. A visualization combined with an affirmation must be vivid, specific and emotionally charged to get effective results. You are encouraged to use these methods of learning to direct your mind to establish new habits of success. This process of mind control is a short cut to reach the unbalanced parenting tapes at alpha and theta levels and to shift these using breath and imagery.

The self-hypnosis process accesses one's mental power to create through thought and spoken word. This is the awakening of abilities that are inherent in each of us. The goal is to relieve pain and disease and to facilitate a core cause relief to avoid a reoccurrence. The hypno-therapist is simply the guide and focusing agent of communication. Maxwell Maltz is a plastic surgeon who studied the reaction of his patients and wrote the book *Psycho-cybernetics* in 1969. He found many of his patients had little or no change of attitude after plastic surgery. Even though their appearance was greatly improved, their self-concept and self-esteem was still low. His research extended to encompass the power of the mind/body link for healing. Dr. Maltz, says "De-hypnotize yourself from false beliefs and learn to utilize the power of rational thinking. Happiness is a habit. Learn to acquire it."

In conscious alert awareness of conversation, a person's mind is in the Beta brain wave frequency. When emotionally distraught, angry or frightened, this is accelerated to high Beta, which is a state of agitation or anxiety. When the person can relax, the brain wave can be lowered into the Alpha brain wave frequency. This is the place where learning takes place and memories are stored. It is the state of intense focused concentration.

In self-hypnosis you go into Alpha, which acts as a bridge to the unconscious. Illogical things may be stored in your unconscious mind because you believed demeaning things about yourself that came from your environment. In self-hypnosis, you will be relaxing into the Alpha brain wave. This is the doorway into the old memories and beliefs. Replace destructive experiences stored in theta by visualizing more constructive ones.

You are in a heightened state of awareness and can come back to Beta at any time you don't like what the hypnosis therapist is suggesting. Before hypnosis session, establish your desired goals. The following is a process to take yourself into the Alpha brain wave frequency:

Self-Hypnosis for Relaxation

Begin the specific restructuring of thoughts by making the affirmations you have planned before the session. The key is to set a special time daily and practice regularly. Bedtime and rising are the best times to treat yourself to a refreshing exercise. Get in a comfortable position with your spine straight, arms and legs uncrossed to facilitate increased energy flow. Begin to concentrate on your breath inhaling to the count of five and exhaling to the count of five. Repeat this breath cycle three times to go into a relaxed state of alpha. With each inhale, visualize that white light is filling you.

On the exhale, visualize yourself as a pressure cooker letting off steam. Repeat this breath cycle three times. Then count out loud slowly backwards from ten to one. With every other count, suggest that you are getting more and more relaxed and receptive to healing as you go deeper and deeper within. Continue gentle relaxed breathing. Imagine that you are floating on a cloud entering your favorite relaxing place. Stay as long as you choose to receive the optimal relaxing effect. This place can be returned to by simply holding the vision of oneself there to restore its relaxing effect. Count from one to five as you return to Beta awareness. 1-2-3-4-5. Move your fingers and toes as you return to the ever vibrant now.

Self-Hypnosis for Cellular Function

Get in a comfortable position with your spine straight, arms and legs uncrossed to facilitate more increased energy flow. Close your eyes and begin to focus on your breath.

Visualize that your conscious mind is enveloped in a peaceful energy to calm and quiet it. Begin to concentrate on your breath. Continue gentle breathing in the quiet zone of relaxing vibrations. As you inhale to the count of five through your nose, visualize luminous white healing energy is filling every cell of your body. Exhale through your mouth to the count of five. Let go of anything that blocks your potential.

This white light has the spectrum of the rainbow colors that go into your cells. Observe this process of healing and hope is going into all your body systems. Repeat five repetitions of this breath cycle and when you finish this cycle go back to the gentle relaxed gentle breathing. Now relax into the process and begin counting slowly backwards from ten to one.

Tell yourself with every count, "I am getting more and more relaxed and receptive to healing as I go deeper and deeper within. Count 10-9-8-7-6-5-4-3-2-1." Visualize yourself in a beautiful place. As you notice sights, smells, sounds and colors of this healing relaxing place, all stress is draining from your face, shoulders and muscles throughout your body. Affirm:

"I am now at level one in a very deep level of peace and relaxation. My mind is working on higher levels of creativity and problem solving. My body is becoming healthier and more efficient. I am aware that the nucleus of every cell throughout my body is filling with an energetic flow of healing. This connects my cellular memory with the image of my perfect body free of all disease from past, present and future. I hold the quality of gratitude for the healing gained. I now come back to Beta awareness on the count of five. 1 – 2 – 3 – 4 – 5. I move my fingers and toes as I return relaxed and rested, united within and without."

Self-Hypnosis for Stress Reduction

A technique in Silva Mind Control presents the following effective procedure:

Close your eyes for this relaxation exercise. Inhale deeply to the count of seven, and exhale to the count of seven to clear your mind. Begin a dress rehearsal of an upcoming situation. Practice how you are going to deal with a stressful situation while remaining in a peaceful state of awareness emotionally. Imagine the details of remaining calm and cool throughout practicing how you would respond, rather than react in the old inappropriate manner. Image yourself in a timeframe after the event has happened and visualized you are telling your friend how smoothly the day has gone and how you were able to conduct yourself in a relaxed manner just as you had in your practice session. In other words, enact a scene looking back on a situation as if you handled it with composure. In your imagery, experience pride of having accomplished this new outcome in the presence of the old triggers. By doing this, you can reprogram your emotional response from pestlets into sprinklets. This whole person healing is directed by your attitude and the way you parent and nurture yourself in beneficial ways.

Affirmations are a form of controlled thought. A visualization combined with an affirmation must be vivid, specific and emotionally charged to get effective results. For an affirmation to work there must be an agreement between the conscious and unconscious mind. Buried guilt and emotions of fear, anger unforgiveness can halt manifestation of success when affirming your intention. Self-hypnosis acts as a bridge between these two parts of your mind to reveal any incongruences. Self-hypnosis has been extremely effective in pain reduction and in regulation of blood pressure and stress. Damage to one's health is caused by reactions. Self-hypnosis can be used to filter certain thoughts such as fear, anger and guilt which depress and slow down the energy field. The mind is at work for the person, or against the person's primary goals whether awake or asleep.

Neuro-Linguistic Programming (NLP)

Neuro-Linguistic Programming utilizes the alpha brain waves of self-hypnosis, It was first defined in the early 1970's at the University of California, Santa Cruz. The practice of NLP utilizes a form of hypnosis to overlay a new memory base over a painful event at the brain wave frequency of alpha. The basic premise of NLP is that the words you use reflect your subconscious perception and this can be changed. It allows you to eliminate the unconscious behaviors and attitudes that get in your way. Remnants of repeated struggles and trauma are removed from your basic thought patterns and energy field. With the restructuring of new foundational thoughts, you can begin to attract a happy, successful life.

Practicing visualization to go into the calmer alpha frequency combines several steps:

The first step sets the overall intention for the desired outcome such as peace in relations, financial security, or right job and location. The second step involves using breath as a bridge to brainwave frequencies of relaxation and balance. The third step utilizes the law of attraction which stipulates to hold the energy of the goal as already accomplished. Imagine how it will feel when the dream has manifested. This draws the chosen result energetically. Rather than setting specifics of goal fulfilment claim, "This or something better." The outcome may be even better than what can be imagined with a limited perspective of unknown events.

By imagining the feelings of fulfillment of goals, a magnetic attraction begins. Projecting the optimistic quality of hope is powerful. Through raising the personal vibrational field with uplifting thoughts, struggles and trauma can be removed from one's core reference and resulting experiences. The important thing is to think about what is wanted, rather than what is feared, because the mind is a co-creator in manifesting desires.

Since every person has the gift of personal will to choose their thoughts and feelings, these decisions create the setting to play out the roles of positive and negative forces. Goal setting activates the energy to accomplish what the person hopes. The power belongs to each person's free will to choose whether to focus on the good, or the bad that is happening within and around them.

By elevating your thoughts and feelings, the benefits of higher vibrations begin to manifest. At first, these may not be understood by the conscious mind. It may seem things are falling apart in this process of change. The old has to be broken down and cleared before the new can be created. Circumstances are unfolding in a new reality in this co-creative experience.

Emotional Freedom Technique and Holy Fire Reiki are processes of shifting energy. Acupressure points and meridians are stimulated energetically to release the flow of life force in these healing arts to bring balance and vibrant health. This aids in shifting the vibration of an organ, system and the whole environment into higher frequencies. New neuro pathways are formed to replace old loops of reoccurring responses. Heartmath is one of the best ways to connect heart brain and head brain for peak mental and intuitive function.

Chapter Three: Integrative Medicine

The Integrative Health concept came out of the view that all body systems are a connected network, and all parts of the whole must be treated to find balance. This is our natural state of health. The Integral Systems approach to health and wellness includes physical and neurological-systems, biological systems, psychological, bio-psychosocial and spiritual/moral aspects of the individual.

Claude Bernard, a brilliant French physiologist and philosopher, coined the term 'homeostasis.' This suggests that a balanced life of good living practices is essential for optimal health and body defense. When attitude and sound nutrition are not in balance, stress results. Stress refers to the consequence of the failure of an organism to respond adequately to mental, emotional, or physical demands, whether actual or imagined.

The term *stress* was first employed in a biological context by the Canadian endocrinologist, Hans Selye, in the 1930s. In his usage *stress* refers to a condition and the term *stressor* relates to the stimulus causing it. This covers a wide range of phenomena, from mild irritation to drastic dysfunction that may cause severe health breakdown. The notion that the nervous system is responsible for several symptoms of illness and disease through the release of stress hormones (epinephrine, norepinephrine, cortisol and aldosterone) was established through his pioneering research. In this theory, stress breaks down the immune response and a dysfunctional immune system can precipitate infection, allergies and serious illness.

Myrin Borysenko is an immunologist at Tuft's University. This research suggests when the autonomic nervous system releases an abundance of stress hormones, several physical repercussions can result such as migraines, ulcers and hypertension. Research applied by Janice Kiecolt-Glaser and Ron Glaser also linked stress to the suppression of the immune system. A 1996 paper revealed chronic stress retards wound healing and accelerates aging.

Before their research it was thought that there was not a direct link between the nervous system and the immune system. Researchers isolated neural endings connecting the Central Nervous System (CNS) to the thymus, lymph nodes, spleen and bone marrow. Thus, these stress hormone receptors are located throughout the body, not just in the brain. Research indicates the shape and behavior of the DNA is related to the functions of the brain. We turned to the brain to understand the mechanisms by which the mind influences the body.

Jo Marchant, author of "Cure: A Journey into the Science of Mind Over Body," gives scientific research to support how the brain can help heal our body. It investigates placebos and the power of positive and negative thoughts to effect of our wellbeing. She relates that our minds have the power to ease pain, fight off infection and slow the progression of serious ailments. The beliefs one holds are critical factors in the process of healing. Research mentioned in her book is showing positive effects with multiple sclerosis, lupus, Crohn's disease and other auto-immune disorders, as well as Irritable Bowel Syndrome (IBS) and arthritis.

Research explains that positive thoughts and beliefs create certain hormones that are supportive to health and negative ones create destructive hormonal responses. When the hormone called cortisol is produced by stress, it turns off the production of the healthy DHEA hormones and organ function.

Another link indicates that neuropeptides (messenger hormones) produced in the brain fit into receptor sites of lymphocytes and are influenced by emotional responses. Candace Pert, former Chief of Brain Chemistry at the National Institute for Mental Health, discovered that throughout the body immune system, cells, not only have receptors for neuropeptides, but they can also manufacture them independently. Her theory also revealed that immune cells have a memory that enables them to adapt to specific emotional responses. Emotions have begun to be a focus of research relating stress hormones breakdown physical and mental functions.

Emotional well-being is the ability to feel and express the entire range of human emotions and to control them. Many health problems are thought to be directly tied to the inability to recognize and appropriately express emotions. Over the last two decades, researchers have begun to realize the importance of the connection of anger to coronary heart disease and cancer, as well as other serious maladies. Only recently, has it been suggested that venting anger creatively brings about improved health.

Humans are the only species that can process anger into delayed revenge and behave aggressively for seemingly inexplicable reasons. Studies indicate that because it has not been socially acceptable for women to express aggressive or violent temperament, these repressed feelings have developed into ulcers, migraines and perhaps breast cancer. Anger is often ignored or suppressed as in depression. Until anger is recognized, it cannot be relieved.

The psychosocial systems of health are affecting class and cultural definitions of one's self in gender roles of men and women. These roles are restructured through balance of expectations of male/female traits. Men were taught to repress emotions as a part of their manhood. It takes unlearning, relearning and implementation to accomplish positive, constructive gains to rid dysfunctional emotions.

Emotions play an important role in modulating body systems that influence our health. Emotions seem to play a crucial part in the genesis and treatment of serious disease such as cancer and other illness. Any kind of unexpected shock can have a devastating effect on health and the immune system. Post-Traumatic Stress Disorder (PTSD) can result.

Living in fear and panic can create biochemical effects that are detrimental to healthy living. One of the first tasks at hand in a successful journey of restoring and maintaining good health is to reestablish the greatest possible measure of inner peace and confidence. The core of this peace comes from focusing on positive emotions of love, joy, peace, hope and gratitude.

Many people are carrying repressed memories of unhealed emotional wounds or traumas from childhood. Having negative thoughts can make the person more disease prone. A study in the journal Proceedings of the National Academy of Sciences links 'negative brain activity' with a weakened immune system. Researchers from the University of Wisconsin-Madison studied people with high levels of brain activity in a region linked to negative thoughts. Those with the highest activity levels responded worse to a flu vaccine. Scientists already knew that pessimists people rated as more sensitive to negative events.

Another approach to creating happiness is the positive psychology researched by Dr. Martin Seligman. in his book "Authentic Happiness: Using the New Positive Psychology to Realize Your Potential for Lasting Fulfillment:" He explains that reliving and recreating the past deters moving on and building a positive future. The time has arrived for a science that seeks to understand positive emotions, builds strength and virtue, and provides guideposts for finding what Aristotle called the good life. Seligman advises to achieve emotional fulfillment and increase one's happiness quotient through incorporating strengths such as humor, originality and generosity into everyday interactions. Picking apart the past trying to solve decade-old problems and fixing weaknesses isn't the most effective method of recovery.

The late Norman Cousins, of UCLA Medical School, described a national survey of oncologists in his last book, *Head First: The Biology of Hope.* In a study on 649 individuals offered their opinions on the importance of various psychological factors in fighting cancer. More than 90% of the physicians said they attached the highest value to the attitudes of hope and optimism. Cousins encouraged people to take preventative action. Chose self-supportive responses and practice them. He recommended to smile and experience the uplifting relaxation that is automatically produced. Laughter lifts the heaviest heart. Implement self-care.

Norman Cousins also advised to change your attitude because it is one thing you do have control over. He expressed many useful suggestions including the following quote:

"Don't let someone else take you to a place you don't want to be. The first step in cleaning up an emotionally toxic environment is to make the choice to find peace of mind and contentment. Be with people who are positive and be one of the positive folks that everyone wants to be with. Make a choice to be in nature every day. Read something inspiring. Challenge your mind with new topics. This helps divert energy to things that empower your inner control. Any toxicity that you relieve in your own life frees you to become a better person and a more productive citizen in the community. Make it your goal to learn to find something to laugh at every day. Take yourself less seriously, as you continue to take your illness and your treatments very seriously."

This advice is consistent with the findings of a recent study showing that method actors asked to generate the emotion of joy within themselves showed an increase in the number of natural killer cells circulating in the blood stream within twenty minutes. A key role of natural killer cells is known to seek out and destroy tumor cells throughout your body. Once the actors got themselves out of this positive state, their levels of natural killer cells quickly dropped again. Joy is the emotion we experience during humor and laughter. These findings indicate that watching a humorous video increases the number of, and activity of, natural killer cells.

Author, Daniel Goleman, has coined the theory he defines as emotional intelligence. He is convinced that learning to identify, empathize and resolve feelings of anger, anxiety, depression (buried anger), pessimism and loneliness is a necessary form of disease prevention. Psychotherapeutic intervention to treat depression includes many coping and relaxation techniques. Meditation and Mindfulness is effective in conjunction with Cognitive therapy.

Studies have shown that physical exercise results in a less depressed state of mind. Integrative health therapies are being consideration by more of the public as more personal responsibility is taken for one's emotions and general well-being. As this trend grows, more people are introspecting their own behavior, looking for alternatives to conventional medicine of prescription drugs and surgery. There is an increasing call for a deeper meaning to life. This has led to the component of a psycho-spiritual whole person system.

Cognitive Behavioral Therapy (CBT) is a psychological approach to stress that includes a variety of approaches and therapeutic systems to treat the whole person. There is empirical evidence that CBT is effective for the treatment of a variety of problems, including mood, anxiety, personality, eating, substance abuse, and psychotic disorders. CBT was developed by Dr. Aaron T. Beck, a psychiatrist in 1960. Albert Ellis developed Rational Emotive Behavior Therapy in the 1950's.

The therapeutic techniques vary within the different approaches of behavior therapy according to the kind of problem. This may include keeping a journal of significant events and associated feelings, thoughts and behaviors. It involves substitution of a positive thought process and analysis of the rational of the validity of the harmful thought process. Relaxation, mindfulness, Neuro Linguistic Programming (NLP) and new target behaviors and reactions are combined with CBT.

Herbert Benson, M.D.is an American cardiologist born in 1935. Benson is a pioneer in mind/body medicine and is one of the first western physicians to bring spirituality and healing into medicine. He is the founder of the Mind/Body Medical Institute at Massachusetts General Hospital in Boston and has authored, or co-author, of more than 175 scientific publications and eleven books. including "Relaxation Response." In his career of over thirty-five years, continues to lead teaching and research into counteracting the harmful effects of stress. His work serves as a bridge between medicine and religion, East and West, mind and body, and belief and science. In his research, the mind and body are one system, in which meditation can play a significant role in reducing stress responses.

The life work of Jon Kabot-Zinn, PhD has been largely dedicated to bringing mindfulness into the mainstream of medicine and society. He received his Ph.D. in molecular biology in 1971 from MIT where he studied under Salvador Luria, Nobel Laureate in medicine. Kabat-Zinn is the founder and former Executive Director of the Center for Mindfulness in Medicine, Health Care, and Society at the University of Massachusetts Medical School. He is also the founder (1979) and former director of its renowned Stress Reduction Clinic and Professor of Medicine emeritus at the University of Massachusetts Medical School.

Jon Kabat-Zinn has written several bestselling books: including "Full Catastrophe Living" and "Coming to Our Senses." His book "The Mindful Way Through Depression: Freeing Yourself from Chronic Unhappiness" is co-authored with J. Mark G. Williams, John D. Teasdale and Zindel V. Segal. It focuses on mind/body interactions for healing. It offers various clinical applications of mindfulness meditation connecting psychology and spirituality to address chronic pain and stress-related disorders. I especially enjoyed the meditations and practical advice in his book, "Wherever You Go, There You Are."

In the early 1900's, Carl Gustav Jung, a psychiatrist from Switzerland, became respected for his influence on modern psychological thought connecting the psychological to the spiritual components of the whole person. Jung developed the theory of the conscious and unconscious mind. He postulated the unconscious mind is the repository of thoughts memories and perceptions that have been dropped from the attention of the conscious mind.

Jung felt that no matter how obscure these ideas and feelings may be, they do not cease to exist and continue to influence thoughts and behaviors. Jung referred to this as the first layer of personal unconscious. He called the second level collective unconscious which is an inexhaustible reservoir of thoughts integrated with ancient wisdom by the collective consciousness of humanity. This has a positive or negative effect on the group as a unit.

Jung claimed this knowledge passed down from generation to generation connecting all people as one in consciousness. Jung believed that although this level was more difficult to access, the resources in this reservoir were invaluable in aiding the self-discovery process. He felt that reluctance, avoidance, and indolence contribute to self-ignorance and perpetuate the stress response. Jung theorized human personality is a process of self-discovery and realization that he referred to as' individuation.' This involves childhood experience that is augmented by a soul search for one's purpose of life.

Jung turned the search inward to explore the depths of the mind, as a means of understanding the spiritual nature of humanity. Jung believed the inability to get in touch with our inner selves has provided fertile ground for life's stressors in modern society. He felt that sickness is a result of not being whole and of never connecting with the qualities of the unconscious mind to clarify values and gain sharp focus on life's meaning.

The late Wayne Dyer, PhD was a psychotherapist who has expanded on Jung's foundational concepts of the personal connection to the whole with a focus on positive thinking and self-actualization. He taught that relaxation is achieved when the present moment is fully experience and appreciated. Yet, as the individual grows into adulthood, the mind becomes willingly preoccupied (often paralyzed) with guilt and anger of the past or fear of the future.

His theories are based on the concept that leftover guilt originates in early childhood as a parenting process to manipulate other people's thoughts, words and actions. This creates a stressful activity of worry which Dyer describes as sitting in the driver's seat without keys, gas or tires. This is an erroneous coping technique in which guilt and worry are distractions from one's ability to start planning strategically for future events. This enables freedom to utilize the full potential of mental and emotional and spiritual resources.

In his book "The Heartmath Solution," Doc Hildre provides an effective manual to use the heart's energy for quality of life and wellness. He is the founder of the Institute of Heartmath in Bouldercreek, CA. The goal of this program is to help the development of heat-brain coherence. His emphasis is in child development, psychotherapy and stress management. The training describes techniques like Quick Coherence and Heart Lock-in to reengineer a person's biochemistry to create the physiology need for peak performance and minimal stress. In his book "Transforming Stress," he has a performance ratio to understand the emotions of the sympathetic and parasympathetic systems and how these relate to the ratio of healing DHEA hormones and cortisol, the stress hormone.

John Freedom has written one of the best books on EFT entitled, "Heal Yourself with Emotional Freedom Techniques." Tapping and stimulating the acupuncture meridians is theorized to remove the blockage and disruption, thereby restoring the free flow of emotional energy. This has been verified by muscle testing to get a stronger response. Tapping on acupoints is believed to desensitize conditioned emotional responses and reassociate a relaxation response. It includes tapping to improve relationships and increasing peak performance. It has been effective in treating fears, performance anxiety, guilt, self-sabotage and other destructive emotional conditions to bring over health and well-being.

Richard J. Davidson, PhD and Sharon Begley are other pioneers in the research of the power of emotions. In their book "The Emotional Life of Your Brain," they describe six continuums that determine a person's 'Emotional Fingerprint' and 'Emotional Style'. their research has shown that each person is a combination of Resilience, Outlook, Social Intuition, Self-Awareness, Attention, and Sensitivity to Context. These are designated by the emotions that are most often felt and regulate the size of related brain centers that originate these specific emotions.

He emphasizes the importance of feeling gratitude for higher levels of energy. Mindful Meditation is an effective way to reduce activation in the amygdala and orbital frontal cortex. This incorporates the process of observing your thoughts, feelings and sensations in the moment in a non-judgmental observation. Techniques are presented to address Autism, Attention Deficit Disorder and Post Traumatic Stress. This is breakthrough research to demonstrate when compassion permeates the whole mind, gamma waves are greater which underlie high mental activity such as consciousness.

Spirituality and Emotions

Author, Aldous Huxley, describes human spirituality as a transcendent reality beyond culture, religion, politics and ego. Spirituality includes aspects of higher consciousness, transcendence, self-reliance, self-efficacy, self-actualization, love, faith, enlightenment, mysticism, self-assertiveness, community and bonding. The World Health Organization (WHO) defines human spirituality as that which is in total harmony with the perceptual and non-perceptual environment. Spiritual reference does not have a religious connotation; rather it refers specifically to the human moral dimension of positive thoughts and feelings.

Typically, people describe their collective spiritual experiences as a journey or path. What is most important for a path is to enhance the maturation, or evolution of the soul. It must be creative, not destructive; progressive, not regressive. The spiritual quality of faith is bringing spontaneous remission to many a life-threatening diagnosis. The medical field is encompassing Integrative modalities of energy medicine, color art, humor, breath, movement, placebo, mind/body and sound therapies.

Human spirituality is defined as the maturation process of our higher consciousness as developed through the integration of three facets: First - an insightful, nurturing relationship with oneself and others; Second - the development of a strong personal value system; Third - a meaningful purpose in life. When these facets are integrated, human consciousness will advance to a higher level of understanding that involves seeing oneself as a part of a larger whole. The world of strife and catastrophes have motivated a collective search called the Human Potential Movement as spirituality becomes a relevant part of Integrative Health.

The speed of this movement has been fueled by a rising interest in ecology and protection of the environment. We are all called to prevent the destruction of our planet. It is important to regulate the sounds, words and thoughts the mind is creating as well as recycling trash. Idle gossip and hateful words are imprints which result in harmful vibrations. The ability to speak is a gift. Use it with responsibility and reverence. Break the illusion of separateness. Each person is not simply doing their own thing; we are all doing everyone's thing. Seek your own inner voice of wisdom to attract the higher vibrations from the stars as you lift to a greater power of strength, beauty and love. In this way, we are each adding to the positive sprinklet energies instead of contributing to the damaging pestlet energies. Reorientation of wording can evoke thoughts of peace, joy and love to create a high field of energy attracting harmonious vibrations and desired outcomes.

The more senses engaged and the more passionate the intention, the better. Setting affirmations (positive statements) to repeated musical rhythms or melodies gives them added vitality. Visualization and guided imagery, with the use of a dominate thought to create a virtual reality must be vivid and specific to get effective changes. A purposeful, deliberate intention is to be emphasized with emotional desire. The natural law of attraction states, "like attracts like." This is accessed to create the desired outcome.

Frequency Shifting

A primary purpose for frequency shifting involves expanding consciousness. This prompts the individual to alter his/her lifestyle and begin to understand the connection to others, to the planet and to the all life. By changing to uplifting vibrations, the disruptive energy often releases naturally, and the imbalance disappears as stored emotional pain is carried away. We are connected to the animals, the plants, the trees and the whole eco-system of nature. When any life form is endangered, it upsets the balance in nature. This imbalance effects our climatic conditions and inner earth status of the fault and lay lines of the earth grids. Until humanity embraces to the act of the Kindness Sprinklet at the 'group consciousness level', we will not be living in balance.

Chapter Four: Character Development

Constructive parenting is the foundation for the building blocks of character development. The educators not only provide early instructions to aide brain behavior, they are role models. The human potential for guiding a young person's life is based in the qualities of the sprinklets. It is critically important to have an attitude to look for the positive lessons in your daily challenges by accepting responsibility for your own choices. Each person's reality is based on their attitude about what has happened. Be a positive role-model and set the standards you want the child to mirror. (For indeed, children repeat what you do.)

Author on personality development, Olivia McIvor writes:

"Speak your truth with honesty and integrity by demonstrating you are as good as your word." When you only say something and don't follow through, it breaks not only peace between you and others, it breaks trust. Compassion is directly related to the ability to speak in ways that can be heard. It is about motivating others to their best potential. By providing a safe supportive environment full of goodwill and respect, you can build character to have the courage to make changes and do what is right even in the face of personal adversity."

"We need to introspect if our words and actions to others motivate, inspire and support, or do they reject, humiliate and condemn. Being tolerant comes when you move from the norm of common ground to higher ground by being able to apologize. All people must come to the place of tolerance and strength in diversity. Kindness starts with a state of mind."

Active listening is a critical factor in optimal parenting skills. It takes being totally present, open and responsive to the words and ideas of another person. Listening is an effective peace building skill. Sometimes all a person needs to make their life turn a corner is to be heard. An anonymous quote relates "We are here to walk each other home." McIvor challenges, "Is there someone in your life or at your workplace who needs someone to walk them home? Until all persons united, we are not living as a global family to build community. We must accept one person can make a difference and ask, What am I doing for others?"

There are great advances in emotional and physical pain management that connect mind body and the spiritual aspects. Dean Ornish, MD reports that one of the most exciting emerging findings in neurosciences in the past decade has been the discovery of what are called 'mirror neurons.' These parts of the brain fire when doing an action and fire the same neurons when observing the same action performed by another person. This is how visualization and guided imagery work to simulate real changes in the body's organ function using simply imagination. If a stressful event is imagined in intricate detail, your arteries constrict, blood pressure increases, blood colts more quickly, muscles tense, breathing rate increases and so on.

The reverse effect takes place on physiological levels when imagining peaceful outcomes. Mindfulness can make us more aware of buried emotions. Dr. Ornish teaches malevolence; he feels that we have not taken the final step of our journey until we cast off the chains of being a prisoner of hatred and live in a way that respects and enhances the freedom of others.

President Bill Clinton echoed these feelings in his 2002 Nigerian parliament address. He said, "Some things you just have to forgive and let go. That's one thing I learned from my friend Nelson Mandela. when I asked him how he forgave those who imprisoned him for so many years." Mandela told President Clinton if he still hated his oppressors when he got outside the prison gate, he would still be their prisoner. He wanted to be free after twenty-seven years of incarceration, and so he let it go. The world will progress as every individual affirms to follow Mandel's example. We will then be free from the negative past and our rehearsal of debilitating thoughts.

Critical depletion of our natural resources is acting as a fire alarm beckoning us to set aside our cultural and political differences and work together as a worldwide people. Dianuid O'Murchu, an Irish priest, teaches the Holy Spirit is the source of all life force and light. In his book entitled, "In the Beginning was the Sprit: Science-Religion and Indigenous Spirituality" he stresses the connection in different dogmas with a call to be fair minded. These are values which our youth need to have instilled.

Winston Churchill advices to create our own universe as we each go along in a joyful, health giving way. Spiritual principals indicate that positive frequencies are much more powerful than the fractured negative dense energetics. The destructive factors cannot take over when people start working together in communities to spread more cohesive communication. Every individual affects the group consciousness of the composite vibrational thoughts to lift the overall energy of our planetary alignment and restore balance in the universe.

Creative Approach to Learning

Optimize Brain Function and Emotional Control

The premise of Creative Learning Programs (CLP), developed by Patrice Joy Harkins is to develop perceptual awareness and motor skills. Stress reduction and other healthy living factors are presented to stabilize the emotions and optimize brain function. The curriculum offers training on confidence building and self-awareness. The first challenge is to identify the child's strengths and weakness. Develop realistic expectations of the child who has learning or emotional issues. Set up opportunities for success in the environment by building on the attributes. These healthy living programs apply to all people, yet they are especially important for those with educational and emotional challenges.

Build Self-Esteem for Optimal Learning

* Assign special chores; feed a pet; help to decorate the house for the holidays.
* Cultivate the child's special interest; go to a museum or start a collection.
* Play with your child and let them direct the game choices.
* Watch for good behavior. Give the child praise, recognition and encouragement.
* View the child as separate from any disability or disruptive behavior.

Target Areas of Consideration

Security – Belief in one's abilities - The parent and authority figures must believe in the child's ability to master a task that is within the child's capacity. Your faith in him/her is encouraging.

Self-motivation – Initiative to begin a task - Never nag or threaten a child. Pressure locks the child into confrontation and patterns of avoidance and procrastination. The underlying motivation is to be concern for the child's well-being and sense of self.

Self-reliance – Dependence on one's self - Let the child make mistakes for this how he/she learns. Encourage effort put forth and reward small steps of improvement.

Self-discipline – Endeavor and effort put forth - Let the child think for him/herself. Let the child help him/herself. Be aware when further directions are needed without interfering.

Motor Skills – Coordination - Muscle development and balance.

Follow through – Ability to finish a task - Let the child finish even if it takes longer so he/she has pride of accomplishment. Praise the child who is doing their best.

Academic Achievement – Skill level - This is commensurate to the child's innate ability and improvement on past effort.

Performance Areas Affected

Start tasks	Make transitions
Stay on tract	Complete tasks
Interact with others	Produce work at consistent levels
Follow-through	Organize multi-tasks

The Best Environment to Optimize Learning Capability

* Provide the child with a structured and predictable environment.
* Display rules; post daily schedules; set specific times for chores; design a quiet workspace.
* Plan academic subjects at the time the child has the highest level of brain function. (Usually this is in the morning).
* Modify curriculum when indicated for learning level, attention span and pace of learning.
* Mix high and low interest activities.
* Teach study skills. (Use 3 x5 note and flash cards). Go over and over the subject matter.
* Establish structure, routines and a predictable environment.
* Do what you say so the child learns your words have meaning.
* Have the child read something of his/her choice and summarize it.
* Immediate consistent consequences encourage the child to continue appropriate behavior.
* Limit demands. Give minimal negative feedback. Provide frequent, plentiful praise.
* Optimize methods of visual or auditory depending on which the child learns more readily.
* Use memory links, key word associations and color codes to focus attention.

Education should be aimed at developing a child's peak learning potential. The child's mental, emotional and physical maturity level are determining factors in the development of this ability. There are three areas that primarily affect this: Self-image, self-reliance and self-discipline. A parent or authority figure can foster these traits in the child by expressing his/her faith and trust in the child's ability and integrity.

A child has a natural curiosity and an instinctive desire to learn. He/she must be encouraged to develop this natural characteristic into the reasoning skills needed in later life. Structure and schedules create an ordered mind and inner discipline. A child will learn more effectively in a relaxed, congenial environment in which interesting topics are presented that relate to his/her main interests.

Allow the child to think for him/herself. This gives the foundation to develop their cognition. Telling the answer before the child goes through the reasoning process of doing the work for him/herself teaches manipulation and co-dependency. Literally a child must learn how to learn. Self-reliance is a key factor in mental mastery. It is easier to do things for a child at first instead of setting up a structure and discipline to get the child to follow through. If work is completed for a child, he/she will not develop trust to rely on themselves.

Respect the suggestion the child offers. If it is not workable, explain why in a respectful manner. Self-motivation is directly related to pride of accomplishment and building the habits of success. Trial and error is the greatest teacher. Effort must be recognized and acknowledged. The child needs to feel secure in an environment of peace and structure so that study habits are part of a planned lifestyle. In this way, the child feels able to accomplish assigned tasks.

If the child is encouraged to do the best he/she can every day, regardless of the results, the productivity of effort increases. If the child is prodded and has too much external pressure to come up with solutions, it can cause a mental shutdown from trying too hard to please. If a child feels he/she must be perfect, it can cause them to be afraid to try at all. The fear of failure negates his//her efforts resulting in discouragement. Disruptive behavior is usually a manifestation of the person's search for attention and appreciation as a human being worthy of love and respect.

Self-reliance cannot be taught by constant external control. The purpose of discipline is to help the child learn to become independent and maintain functional, appropriate behavior. Self -reliant living skills require that responsibility is given in measured amounts. If the child does not carry out the instructions, he/she has a favorite privilege removed. The concept is that rewards and freedom come in direct proportion to responsibility assumed in life. For example: If the child doesn't do his/her homework, TV or another privilege is lost for the night. This is the way the world functions. Adults get rewards for work and lose benefits if they won't work.

Self-discipline is trained by consequence of action. If the child does not assume responsibility, he/she should have a privilege removed. Consistency is vital. Children can use control mechanisms to prove they can't do the work or make it difficult for the parent to persist:

1. Dawdling
2. Acting incompetent and sloppy work
3. Laughing and joking when it is time to work
4. Acting if consequences and restriction don't bother him/her
5. Lack of respect with arguments or hateful words
6. Not listening

Build a Positive Self-Image

A positive self-image is necessary to be secure enough to become independent. The way a person handles his/her angry emotions is a factor in forming a good self-image. Training a child to handle anger is accomplished by mirroring the adult's pattern in this process. A person can only be in balance when inner control is maintained. To do this, one must not allow others to get by with control games. When the parent maintains balance within, this is mirrored and the child benefits.

Children are masters at learning how to control a situation and push our buttons. A child watches an adult lose control and repeats this unhealthy response. In this case, self-respect is not fostered, and the child learns controlling behaviors.

Establish Constructive Work Habits

Children are great imitators. They will listen to you to the extent you listen to them. Tell the child what you want them to do, rather than what you don't want. For example: Tell the child: "Close the door quietly," rather than, "Don't slam the door." Establish responsibility at an early age. Post a schedule of a time to do specific task like chores and homework. Then delegate the responsibility to the child to remember. If an assigned project is not completed when the work should have been done, the child is then reminded he/she must complete the task, but still loses a privilege. This motivates the child to remember on their own. It is best to keep all discipline within the day of the offense. Each day is a clean slate.

Build Self-Confidence

The object in building healthy self-esteem is to get the child to see negative behavior as a separate part of him/herself which can be corrected. This is not related to being loved for this is given unconditionally. Respect the child's feelings. Expect cooperation. No child has ever decided in anger, or resentment to become a better person. This decision is only made by a rational understanding of oneself through the faith others have in you.

Treat the child as a person, not a problem. There is a fine line of distinction between disapproval of the action, but not disapproval of the child him/herself. Avoid giving restriction when angry and emotionally distraught. It may be out of proportion to the offense and cause defiance, rather than cooperation. Only compare the child's actions with earlier attempts. Use him/her as their own yardstick of measurement for improvement. Never compare to a sibling.

A child needs the freedom to have their own opinions and interests to build his/her confidence. Avoid arguing with the child. When you win, you lose. You always lose respect of your authority and the relationship suffers. Be honest with the child. If the work needs improvement, don't say it is fine. Don't ridicule the child for poor work. Simply say what needs correcting and more effort is needed to finish the project. Any mind can be reached more effectively with a steady loving force, rather than harsh analytical logic or abusive condemnation. Play time and cuddle time are the most important things a parent can share to make happy childhood memories and foster self-worth and sufficiency. Love lights the path for learning.

Establish Emotional Balance

Balancing emotions is part of the developing learning capability. If a person lives in a continual state of stressful emotion, the body systems break down, as well as mental capability. Patterns of chronic environmental pressures result in a decline in mental function and physical health. The emotions of anger, fear and guilt are the most prevalent emotions that cause this stress. When the cortisol stress hormone is produced, it affects other hormonal functions. Changes take place in the body's chemical balance resulting in lower brain and organ function.

We are each in control of the world we create by the choices we make. Choosing to focus on positive aspects that are self-supportive leads the individual to **set** boundaries. Thus, the person forms new relationships which aid harmony and replacement of struggle and self-judgment. The emotional response of anger usually goes back to earlier experiences of association, lack of personal power and safety. Awareness is the first step to stop this pattern.

All emotions hold a vibration. Peaceful and joyful energy is supportive to optimal, clear thinking and better health. Emotions of anger, fear and guilt drain energy and destroy health of mind, body and spirit. Everything has a vibrational rate and the "Law of Attraction" sorts out matching vibrational frequencies. Our feelings tell us what vibrational frequency we are tuned to. They return to you precisely what you are putting out. Our words attract what we can expect. For example: A person can draw the very thing they focus on by worrying about being ill and repeatedly using the phrase, "I am sick and tired of _____," By concentrating on failure, the process can be set in motion. If a person continually fears failure, they can shut down their brain function and mental clarity. This becomes a self-fulfilling prophecy.

Reorientation of wording can evoke thoughts of peace, joy and love to create higher vibrations of energy attracting harmonious energy and desired outcomes. Consistent love and support create a solid environment for learning to take place Give the child a sense of acceptance and belonging. Never assume someone knows you love them without being told regularly. Encourage the child by giving genuine compliments. For instance: Tell the child, "Good job, I am proud of you." Give eye to eye contact and engage by being fully present with your child. If you are distracted or resentful of time spent with one another, the child feels this rejection. Be emotionally available for your child. Set limits and consistent rules.

Thought replacement is the key to stabilizing a supportive emotional base. In this process, one gains personal empowerment and is controlled from within, rather than from without. A person is either living in the driver's seat, or passenger seat being driven by influences outside of one's self. Many times, these driving forces are distractions from the past, or guilt which is projected from the actions of others, or fears that are imagined. Whether real or imagined, it is not functional to carry this baggage around. It distracts mental focus and affects concentration and memory.

Chapter Five: Avoid Destructive Parenting Processes

Completely avoid the following behaviors:

- Ordering, threats, physical violence
- Backing down or not following through
- Giving up on expecting the child to do required work
- Becoming so stress by your own problems you are not consistent with the child
- Disconnection due to crisis that interrupts the bond with the child
- Trying to find fulfilment in the child creating a smothering type of bond and neediness
- Overprotection and making the child feel inept
- Excessive fear for the child's safety creates insecurity at the foundational level.
- Giving in to the child out of guilt. (This can be from losing your temper or ignoring the child.)
- Shielding the child of natural consequences of his/her actions
- Too many sedentary hours watching TV and gaming
- No time for interactive play with the child
- Violence of all forms

Inappropriate Behavior

Give the child one warning that the behavior is inappropriate. Give two reminders and if the harmful behavior continues, he/she will have a restriction. Ignore all comments, promises and arguments by the child. Attention on disruption only encourages pestlet behavior. Carry through the restriction that is appropriate. This would mean limiting the next thing they were going to get as a treat. Implement with peace and patience. For example: "Since you _____, you won't get to go over to your friend's house today."

Train Emotional Control and Self-Respect

Develop Good Listening Skills

The child may have poor listening skills due to several factors: It can simply be poor habits of not paying attention, but it could be that he/she is blocking verbal input from patterns of verbal abuse. If verbal stimuli is caustic, harsh, vexatious and angry, absorption of information could be affected. Yelling at the child teaches him/her not to listen. Lower voice tones carry authority. The parent or authority figure needs to bring the child's misconduct to his/her attention. This can be done in a firm, yet nurturing tone. The less words, the better. Be concise! Nagging causes resistance in the child. The goal is to prepare a ready receptacle within the child who is perceptually, emotionally and mentally mature.

The first rule in training self-respect and control: Be Kind!

Effect of Stress on the Learning Process for the Challenged Child

Control of emotions is also a factor in developing one's learning ability. Emotional distress is a valid form of stress. Stress created from a lack of safety affects learning capacity. The parent can help the child channel his/her anger without directing it at another person. The child should not be told to shut down or bury frustration within. A place should be established away from other people in which the child can go and express his/her anger. This could be called an *unhappy place*, or pe*stlet room* in a seclude area. This is not to be in their bedroom.

The child should be counseled to utilize a process to avoid being angry with him/herself regarding mistakes or failures. Guilt is a negative emotional process that need to be replaced with acknowledgement and action. The child must first become open to recognize when his/her behavior is thoughtless or careless. If he/she is taught that this behavior is cruel, or the child is a bad person, the guilty feelings get repressed instead of dealt with at the time.

The goal is for the child to become an observer of his own thoughts, feeling and actions. By facing them, they can be shifted to constructive outcomes. If a child is shamed for mistakes or misbehavior, he/she will incorporate anger at self and authority figures. Guilt and game playing can result. Many people, big and little, hide their faults from themselves because of heavy condemnation as a child.

Remember that a child under stress may make learning difficult. Instead of using phonics to sound out a word, he/she might start trying to think what the word is or may look at another part of the page to relate it to the picture. Afraid of making a mistake on the word, the child may try to figure it out in context to the rest of the words in the sentence, or in the story. With all this going on at the same time, he/she could stumble on the word, or hesitate, and get fearful. This clouds the thinking process even more because it sends blood, oxygen and energy to my extremities instead of my brain.

The child may feel guilty and insecure. All these emotions cloud his/her reasoning capacities. Then this child may begin to start thinking he/she is stupid and then just get mad at him/herself, the failure and the situation. Sometimes a child tries too hard and other times a child is afraid to try at all. If this happens, the child is faced with realizing their failure.

Chapter Six: Balancing the Hemispheres of the Brain

One of the key factors in optimizing brain function is the balancing of the masculine aspects of protective guidance and the feminine aspect of nurturing to become a complete person within through your relationship to self and to others. The following imagery helps in integrating your left brain and your right brain function to facilitate this whole brain utilization. This brings the balanced parental roles of mother and father together. This aids more access to mental acuity and clarity. This is a key factor for those of all ages to have optimal intelligent and emotional access. It is said that humanity is only using 10% of our mind's capacity. More of the other 90% can be accessed by uniting the qualities of your left/brain logic masculine traits and your right/brain creativity feminine traits. Activate the male and female qualities of brain function within yourself in the following meditation: (You can read the following imagery with your child to activate whole brain function.) Get in a quiet place with calm music.

Balancing Left/Right Brain (Male/Female) Function

As you inhale to the count of five through your nose, visualize luminous white healing energy is filling every cell of your brain. Exhale through your mouth to the count of five letting go of destructive thought patterns, behaviors and beliefs. Repeat this breath cycle five times….

Focus the awareness that the two hemispheres of your brain are functioning in coordination. This creative force field is realigning the DNA and cellular memory base into your perfect blueprint of wholeness. Your heart, mind and body are united and connect as the *One*. Affirm: "We are all one at the level of our love." ……

Express the following: "I have gratitude for the healing gained. I now come back to beta awareness on the count of five. 1 – 2 – 3 – 4 – 5. I move my fingers and toes as I return relaxed and rested, united within and without.

Develop Unlimited Reasoning of Left-Brain Capacities

The left/brain controls analytical reasoning and logic. It involves objectivity and rational action. Assertive action and speaking out firmly are activities of balanced left/brain.

This is a description of optimal left/brain function: Gather related information to a problem you wish to solve. Let it incubate for at least thirty minutes without letting your intellect interfere. Begin the process of free association to connect stepping-stones with the solution. Allow a random flow of thoughts to reach a higher conclusion. (Involve three people in this brain storming process for best objectivity).

Balancing Left/Right Brain Function:

There is a line which divides the left and right parts or hemispheres of the brain called the midline. Nerve transmission from the left side of the brain controls the right side of the body crossing the mid-line and the right side of the brain controls the left side of the body.

Activities that activate the brain pattern of crossing the mid-line:

1. While marching, touch your hand to the opposite knee.
2. Swim turning your head to the right while making a stroke with the left arm and then repeat the same on the right side.
3. Crawl for five minutes.
4. Do a yoga breathing technique: Hold your right nostril closed and breath in through the left side of your nose to the count of seven; hold to the count of seven; hold your left nostril closed and exhale to the count of seven out the right nostril; inhale through the right nostril to the count of seven; hold to the count of seven; close your right nostril and exhale through the left nostril to the count of seven. Close with a deep cleansing breath with both nostril open. Repeat this balancing exercise three times daily.
5. Movement through dance, walking, skipping, exercising also involves the whole brain by activating both left and right hemispheres of the brain/body connection.

The Power of Affirmations

Constructive affirmations are a positive present moment statement that do not state what will happen later, but what process you desire to draw into your experience at the current time. A person can state a harmful affirmation such as "I am dumb, or I can't do this." This has a powerful co-creative effect to bring this undesired outcome of failure and low self-esteem. The mind is like a computer and doesn't have a timeline. It acts on what is programed and does not respond to future tense actions. State a desired affirmation and visualize this affirmation as already true in your life as Then you create a magnetic effect to bring the future into the present. The brain follows the intent to either clarify or to shut down from harmful affirmations. Sprinklets or pestlets will control the outcome.

Developing Creativity of the Right Brain

The right/brain has intuitive, artistic and creative function and is connected to one's feelings. It is the ability to receive, but a person can shut down the process of receiving due to lack of self-love. If it hurts too much to feel, the person simply stops as a matter of self-defense. It is important to open up to only the highest form of love and establish boundaries to painful input to restore this ability to receive. This is the only way to move beyond any repressed emotions of guilt or being undeserving to experience life's bounty and success. Nature is a pathway into the functions of the right brain.

Practice the following imagery before a creative project:

- ✱ Be the wind. Run with a veil blowing in the breeze. Imagine you are a butterfly.
- ✱ Now you are floating on a cloud. Be a raindrop. Now you are a moonbeam.
- ✱ Connect with the beauty of a flower and take in its essence and fragrance.
- ✱ Go outside and hug a tree and ask it to share its wisdom. Follow its root system and go down into the Earth core where all knowledge is connected......
- ✱ Allow the Earth to absorb any trouble and negativity as you exhale....
- ✱ On the inhale, fill your mind with clarity.
- ✱ Let your heart connect to the heart of the tree and fill with its wisdom.......
- ✱ Follow the sounds in nature and go into the sound of silence.........
- ✱ Be the sunshine in the lives of others as you beam out this healing light..........

Art Therapy

Another very effective right brain coping technique is art therapy which involves drawing a picture to represent a metaphor of a feeling or life event. This can also be a picture of a familiar house, a relationship or a time in life. This creative process utilizes the language of the unconscious mind which express in colors, symbols and abstracts. Color therapy associates specific healing qualities derived from the color's vibration.

Each person has an 'Inner Child' stored within. Deeply buried trauma or joy can be accessed from the inner child's stored memory bank. Draw pictures of the sprinklets and pestlets that are held in this memory bank (holding tank). Each color used in a drawing holds an opportunity for awareness and emotional release. These allow the attached emotions to be freed without reliving events that might be too painful to hold in the conscious mind. Art accesses the nonverbal communication and symbols stored in the unconscious memory The following are hypnotic exercises to access this same memory base stored deep within.

Finding Solutions

Techniques from Silva Mind Control

Close your eyes. Use your breath to relax.

Inhale to the count of five and exhale to the count of five.......

Visualize a stage with closed curtains. Draw open the curtains and see your problem being enacted for a brief moment. Now see the curtains close ending your connection to the problem. Take in three deep breaths which bring the solution. Release all else on the exhale and don't visualize the problem again. Clear all thought other than the upcoming solution. Now imagine the curtains open again revealing the answer to your original problem. Watch this enacted as you inhale three times. Anchor this answer into every cell of your body. Release the result into a bubble of unconditional love rising into higher realms to bring about the plan of rectification. Close the curtain in your mind, trusting you will know when to take the next step.

… Styles of Learning: "How Children Learn" by Thomas Armstrong

Linguistic – Children with this kind of intelligence enjoy writing, reading, telling stories or doing crossword puzzles.

Logical Mathematical – Children with this kind of intelligence are interested in patterns, categories and relationships. They are drawn to math, strategy games and computers.

Body Kinesthetic – These children process knowledge through body sensations. They are often good at sports and my become actors or craftspeople.

Spatial – These children think in images and pictures. They may spend time with jigsaw puzzles, mazes, legos, blocks and daydreaming.

Musical – These children are good communicators and have interpersonal intelligence. They seem to understand other's feelings and may grow into teachers, counselors or salespeople. They learn by interacting with others.

Interpersonal – Children with this kind of intelligence may be shy. As adults they may be writers, poets or creative business owners. They think outside the box.

There is also Solitary style of learning, which is Intrapersonal. This is when a child learns as they consider things introspectively.

Face Fear

Fear can be allowed to dominate a person's life, just as much of our world lives in a state of generalized fear. The tendency to handle this overload can be to wall off one's self from these threats which are on personal and global levels. Rather than critically deny what you are experiencing, or shutting down, it is important to work with her emotions by recognizing and letting harmful feelings flow away. A person can see upsets as opportunities to respond in new ways, rather than be the victim of one's reactions and fears.

A healthy mental framework includes informed awareness of real risks which keep the individual from a destructive act or lifestyle. Without any fearful emotional response, we would have no barometer to decipher potential harm. On the other hand, paranoia takes over when fear is out of balance to reality. This can lead to debilitating irrational or unrealistic anxiety and become one's prominent mood.

When the person is locked in avoidance and repression, anxiety can create other health problems which lead to chronic stress disorder. This behavior can lead to serious consequences. The following self-hypnosis program is a plan to intervene with this. The outcome goal of this self-hypnosis-process is to become internally directed by truth. It can address fears of public humiliation or vulnerability in intimacy.

Step One: *(Get in a quiet place and practice this process.) Close your eyes* and relax as you count slowly backward from ten to one. Visualize that you are going deeper within separating from disturbing fears. 10...9...8...7...6...5...4...3...2...1.

Step Two: Give yourself an auto-suggestion in this relaxed state, "I respond in only healthy ways to all concerns. I let go of all imaginary fears".

Step Three: Imagine all your illusionary fears are wrapped neatly in a bundle and tie this closed. Put this bundle of false fears inside the basket of a hot air balloon and watched it lift into the air. As it rises out of sight, affirm, "I let all illusionary fears go into the wind."

Step Four: Next, affirm this autosuggestion: I have found a center of peace with the courage and self-confidence to be open to life. "At the count of five, I will be filled with courage and prepared to cope with a truth-based reality. At the count of five, I will be alert, awake, aware to begin new opportunities and adventures." 1...2...3...4...5.

The parent will not lose authority if his/her child realizes that their parent also makes mistakes and is growing and trying. It is an excellent example to set for the child when he/she can see the parent endeavoring to become a better person who respects others and who continues to improve. If a parent builds respect of their self and for the child, this is what the child learns. The more kindness, consideration and consistently a child is taught, the easier it will be to teach self-discipline. The decision to be considerate is only made with a compassionate, understanding of oneself and empathy for others.

The Process of Building Skill Levels in Education

An environment of firm, consistent structure provides the basis for learning. Pride of accomplishment is a key factor in self-reliance. If a child feels good about their accomplishments, they will be motivated to try again. If his/her efforts are ignored, criticized, or thwarted, they can become discouraged. Children have an instinctive desire and curiosity to learn. A child must be encouraged to develop these natural characteristics. Allowing the child to think for him/herself provides the foundation to develop analytical reasoning. Self-acceptance and personal development depend on recognition from those the child loves and respects.

SECTION TWO

The Parent's Role

Chapter Seven: Constructive Parenting of Self and Others

According to the theory of Transactional Analysis (TA), every person has three parts in their mind which store supportive and destructive memories, attitudes and beliefs. Whether a person is big or little, he/she is said to have a parent, child and an analyst aspect their mind. The mind acts as a tape recorder in which all of the things that have been said are recorded in tapes. The *parent mind* records tapes that relate to rules, manners, safety standards, work ethics, social norms and behaviors. Some of these are supportive parental tapes are the fraternal protective guidance system. Others are the maternal tapes of kindness and nurturing. This balanced system trains responsibility and maturity. Self-discipline, structure, virtues and integrity are behaviors trained in the balanced *parent mind* tapes. A responsible approach to life is at the core of balanced parent mind tapes.

Some are harmful imbalanced tapes in the *parent mind* are caustic berating, nagging, critical judgmental words that bully and suppress self-worth. These are verbally and emotionally abusive. As an adult, a person tends to parent him/herself and others in the way they were parented. These result in hot buttons that can trigger reactions from childhood.

The balanced constructive tapes of the *child mind* form childhood can be joyful, curious, spontaneous, adventurous, loving, hopeful, grateful, peaceful, honest and kind sprinklets. Rest and relaxing activities, as well as a core attitude to life that is fun loving and light-hearted are centered in the *child mind*. Some of the unbalanced harmful tapes stored in the *child mind* are fear, anger, rage, guilt, depression, smug, sadness, loneliness, worry, grief and dishonesty pestlets. These are based on life experience and resulting feelings and thought processes. A child discovers him/herself by the parent's reaction to them. The 'inner child' in those of all ages is formed by the overall environment.

The balanced *analyst mind* is the analytical reasoning faculty of open objectivity. It has the capacity to discern if a thought or feeling is of value and in the person's best interest. The *analyst mind* can be used to analyze the person's belief system and the concepts that are in the parent tapes. This part of the mind can also be used to analyze what the parent mind is thinking and what the child mind is feeling. It can shift a harmful pestlet feeling to a positive sprinklet one. A person using the *analyst mind* in an unbalanced manner can become caught in stereotyping, assumptions and conclusions about a situation without looking at all the related facts. The person can acquire attitudes regarding gender, race, religion or age related that limit and label behaviors and capabilities.

The TA theory is helpful in self-awareness to determine what aspect of your mental/emotional aspects you are focused on. Is it balanced adult, child and analyst, or is it the unbalanced functions of these parts of your whole being? There is a time for utilizing all three of the balanced parts of one's wholistic nature. Mark Widdowson has written the book a book entitled, "Transactional Analysis: 100 Key Points and Techniques." It is a modern book written on theory and practice that is especially helpful to parents. It is a trouble shooting guides to avoid common pitfalls that many individuals in life management skills.

The following is a chart of the aspects of balanced and unbalanced behavior in those of all ages.

Balanced Parent Mind	Unbalanced Parent Mind
Flexible	Rigid
Guiding	Manipulative
Gentle	Domineering
Kind	Harsh punishment
Patient	Abusive, cruel, violent
Parameters	Entrapment
Nurturing	Neglectful

Balanced Analyst Mind	Unbalanced Analyst Mind
Objective	Critical
Discerning	Judgmental
Logical	Cold and Calculating

Balanced Child Mind	Unbalanced Child Mind
Playful	Bored
Trusting	Fearful paranoia
Innocence	Pessimistic
Spontaneous	Regimented
Complete absorption	Fragmented concentration
Enthusiastic zest	Nihilism

Attributes of the Balanced Parent - Analyst – Child Traits

Traits from Ages One to Five

These build the process of rational thought, problem solving skills, self-confidence and self-motivation. The following list teaches what a child learns in balanced everyday interactions with authority figures from ages one to five:

Encouraging language skills – Perquisite's for learning pronunciation and social skills

Toilet Training – Self –control and pride

Crawling – Left/right brain function for academic skills and dexterity

Picking up own mess – Tidiness, order and responsibility

Kind Touches – Trust and affectionate behavior

Fair and appropriate discipline – Self-discipline from consequence of action

Listening – Concentration and focused attention

Consistency – Teaches perimeters, stability and sense of security

Efficient work habits – Time efficiency, pride of accomplishment

Regulated Schedule – Boundaries and structure

Healthy eating habits - Good health, calm/ stable moods, pleasant disposition,

Outcome of Balanced Parenting

Brings out the best qualities through validation

Provides a gentle guidance system of values

Creates a safe environment of protection

Gives a capacity to view objectively

Aids clear choices in decision making

Instills lighthearted approach to life

Fosters creativity and sensitivity

Develops capacity to see all as equal

Establishes a habit of praise of self and others

Destructive Traits Fostered by Unbalanced parent/analyst/child Traits

Judgement – Teaches self-criticism and to be comparison oriented and judgmental of others.

Lack of boundaries – Trains lack of respect for others needs and property

Martyrdom – Fosters resentment, guilt and self-sacrifice patterns

Shielding child from all adversity – Inability to handle difficulty and lack of responsible habits

Over permissive - Manipulative personality

Inconsistency – Insecurity and lack of structure

Overindulgent - Waste and extravagance

Over concern with injury- Fearful approach to life and equation of love with worry

Pity – Confusion with pain/pleasure responses; tendency to equate love with suffering

Violent TV – Desensitization to violence and creates a lack of reality of acts of violence

Resulting Behavior of Unbalanced Parenting of Self and Others

Feelings of being attacked, needing to defend

Feeling violated, unloved and being treated unfairly

Feeling inferior or superior to others, game playing

Tendency to overreact, attack and criticize others

Repressed behavior of withdrawal (shy and shamed)

Aggressive behavior of verbal and physical attack

Feelings of undeserving, guilt and self-punishment

Belief in scarcity, limitation and excuses

Defiant rebellion, abusive, cruel treatment of others

Getting stuck in harmful, codependent relationships

Addiction to drugs, alcohol, oral fixations about food

Dishonesty, denial projection, delusions, blaming

Confused thinking' depression, negativism

Fearful, rigid, inflexibility, control issues of self/others

Overdeveloped sense of responsibility/consciousness

Loss of ability to feel and experience emotions

Approval seekers who loose own identify

Isolated people afraid of authority figures

Confusion of love and pity

Victims and rescuers

These outcomes were probably not the things the parent set out to train their child. Yet, it is what happens in with cause and effect. The harsh truth is the child has the first eighteen years to prepare for life. When and who will be the teacher if not the balanced parent? If a person doesn't have supportive early parenting, he/she can become their own nurturing guide. This is accomplished by providing a place of safety in a kind, gentle manner.

Rather than following the example of intimidating harsh and judgmental parenting, patient respect directs the treatment of this wounded child. Leave the old patterns of self-recrimination behind. No longer look at oneself through the eyes of others who were dysfunctional authority figures. Assume the authority located in the balanced three minds within. Be the balanced 'New Parent' and balanced 'Wise Analyst' to the balanced liberated child. Use meditation and breathing practices to overcome crisis mode living to improve communication based on mutual respect.

Destructive Parenting Styles of Self and Others

The following is a list of the behaviors that can result from unbalanced parenting during childhood and earlier years. The most formative years are ages one to five:

Nagging, coercive parent:
o This can lead to defiance and depression.
o This can also lead to a docile adult who continues to need to be told what to do and procrastinates.

Overprotective parent:
o This can lead to a withdrawn adult who can't take initiative.
o Shielding the child form all adversity teaches an inability to handle difficulty and lack of responsible behaviors. When a parent is overly concerned with injury, it teaches a fearful approach to life and equation of love with pity and pain. When a child is protected from the consequence of their actions, they fail to develop maturity.

Overindulgent parent:
o This can lead to an impulsive adult who expects others to wait on them.
o Continual instant gratification teaches lack of maturity and a false sense of expectancy.
o When a parent gives in and never says "No", it trains the traits of a manipulative personality.
o If the parent doesn't train the child to pick up their won messes, It leads to an adult who isn't responsible for his/her environment.

Martyred parent:
o This fosters resentment, guilt and self-sacrifice patterns.
o This trait can be confused with a demonstration of love.

Inconsistent parent:
o This can lead to an adult with insecurity and lack of structure.
o This can train the lack of perimeters, stability and pride of completion.

Perfectionist parent who withholds praise:
o This can lead to an adult who is a perfectionist.
o This can also lead to an adult who is an overachiever.
o This can also lead to an adult who continually needs to prove their worth.

Absentee parent (either mentally, emotionally or physically):
o This can lead to an adult who has trouble with commitment.
o This can lead to an adult who feels, insecure, invisible and is one who is not seen or recognized.
o This can lead to an adult who feels he/she is unwanted and unlovable with low self-esteem.

Critical parent:

o This can lead to an adult who is guilt ridden, bitter and hostile.
o This can lead to a demanding adult who never gets enough proof of love

Permissive parent:

o This can lead to an adult who doesn't respect the needs of others.
o This can lead to an adult who takes advantage of other's boundaries.

Bigoted and prejudice parent:

o This can teach a lack of tolerance for those different than oneself.

Domineering parent:

o This can lead to an adult who is controlling of others or submissive in relationships.

Cruel abusive parent:

o This can lead to an adult who is abusive, or who gets a mate who treats them like the parent.
o This can lead to an adult who has distrust, fear and a withdrawal from reality.

Overloaded, thoughtless parent

o A child can be treated in a neglectful, disrespectful manner. An example of this is when a child is dragged by one arm as the parent hurries along. Rushing creates extreme anxiety. Family members are challenged to prioritize their daily activities to cut down overload.

Judgmental parent:

o This can lead to an adult who has self-devaluation patterns.
o This can teach self-criticism and to be judgmental and comparison oriented.

Jealous parent:

o This can lead to an adult who is jealous and feels their mate needs to be to prove their love.

Balanced Parenting Questionnaire

The following is a self-help questionnaire to counter the detrimental effects of unbalanced parenting processes. These could be ways the person was parented as a child by parents, guardians, or authority figures. It could be results of the ways those in their social network interacted with the person in school, work and personal relationships as they got older. It can also the unbalanced ways the person has parented themselves to carry on the disruptive parenting patterns. This self-evaluation is not meant to replace needed medical or psychological consultation. A person either holds the power of self-control or gives this power away. The goal is to determine how to create a more fulfilling life for oneself filled with sprinklets. This series of questions offer an introspective tool to re-evaluate attitudes and behaviors that are not in the person's best behalf:

Transactional Analysis (TA) and Relationships

Here is a process to utilize TA theories to optimize success in personal control, relationships and goal attainment for oneself and for the family:

1. Continue to use the analyst mind to discern your thoughts and emotions:
2. Realizing each person has done the best he/she can with the programming they had growing up, be more forgiving of yourself and others.
3. List your hot buttons and upsetting reactions.
4. Determine which part of the unbalanced mind has repressed these tapes.
5. Make the intention to regulate these for optimal living skills:
6. Use your breath to relax into the alpha brain wave where memory takes place.

Constructive Tools for Self-Parenting

The key to correcting the unbalanced effects is to recognize them and make an intention to stop parenting one's self in these ways. There is a tendency to carry on dysfunctional parenting from one's youth. This continues from one generation to another. The following are ways to stop these pestlet patterns and to start parenting yourself in loving sprinklet ways:

Make a list of desired behaviors. Practice reading these aloud daily to affirm the new goals. Use diligence in catching any self-talk that is not supportive. Change your reaction to the abusive relationships that are still going on in your environment. If possible, open up communication with other individuals involved. Find, demonstrate and maintain a firm *Wise Analyst* voice to protect yourself and claim humane, balanced interactions.

Self-Questionnaire

— Do I give myself away to negativity?
— Do I live in inner conflict or peace?
— Do I give myself away to grievances and forgiveness?
— Do I give myself away in invalidation?
— What areas do I want to change to recover my personal power and find contentment?
— Do I accept other people's opinion of me without question?
— Do I lose myself by stereotyping?
— What do I believe about the major role models and authority figures in my life? These include Mother, Father, Brother Sister, Grandparents, Aunts, Uncles, Teacher and Boss.
— Do I lose myself living in the past or in the future?
— Do I honor my time? Do I give my time to the things that bless and enrich me?
— Do I have a balance of work, play and rest?
— Am I living in the present moment by thinking about what I am doing?
— How can I experience what I am doing more completely?
— Do I protect and nurture my inner child with balanced parenting?
— Do I honor myself by setting reasonable boundaries?
— Do I live in fantasy, in fairytale dreams, or in reality?
— Am I being codependent expecting others to fix my problems for me?

Balanced Activities to Improve Quality of Life

* Think of enjoyable ways of relaxing. Choose one and do it.
* Make an appointment for a massage.
* Exercise doing something active that you enjoy.
* Begin something you have been tying up energy by putting it off.
* Stop doing everything and just "be" for a while.
* Make a list of the things you are grateful for in your life.
* Scream! Beat a pillow!
* Think of a goal that will bring you joy. Set up a plan to accomplish it.
* Resolve to free yourself from fear and anger. Do this by centering on your strengths.
* Arrange a meeting with your favorite person. Get out and go someplace special.
* Give something away.
* Tell someone you love him or her.
* Make a list of things you feel guilty about.
* Consider where you can make amends and let it go.
* Plan a surprise for someone.
* Clean up something.
* Organize a part of life that has been producing irritation.
* Declutter your house and your mind.
* Check to see if your life is out of balance in regard to play, work and rest.
* Relax by a cozy fire.
* Listen to the wisdom in silence in nature.
* Smile and experience its uplifting quality of joy. Laugh with someone.
* Read something inspiring to divert your mind and inspire your heart.

Gestalt is another effective form of problem solving through the physical release of emotions with physical movement, rather than suppressing them. Beat a pillow or scream to get the energy moving that has held the unbalanced parent programming in the bondage of tortured thoughts and feelings. Exercise and expressive dance are tools to move energy and thus release blocked emotions. Movement is another path to forgiveness. When implementing these coping techniques, a person triggers a time of self-discovery which brings *incorporation* of the new insights based on the balanced parenting process of the *Wise Analyst*.

Create the Joy You Desire by Focusing on Sprinklets

The phrases that are repeated by one generation after another are part of the unbalanced parenting system. When a person believes a negative saying, the process of cause and effect can become a self-fulfilling prophecy. Examples of negative proclamations:

"If anything can go wrong, it will."

"If it isn't one thing, it's another."

"All good things come to an end."

This creates patterns of destructive thoughts and consequences of unbalanced parent tapes. Positive thinking advocates and scientists have proven the creative power of thoughts and words. Stress patterns from the negative emotions which follow negative thinking, result in biochemical changes that are destructive to every gland and organ in the body. In an escalating process of decline, blood pressure becomes elevated and aging takes place as cells become toxic and the immune system breaks down. Positive affirmations can redirect this process to work on one's behalf. Instead of living as the stress-filled victim, begin to build joy.

A pattern of low self-esteem that fosters negativity, frustration and powerlessness causes defensiveness and blaming others for weaknesses. Denial of one's emotions restricts the expression of them. If it has not been ok as a child be upset or cry, then the person only allows themselves to experience a numbing emotional effect.

Experiencing one's good qualities builds a positive self-concept and enables the person to accept their full range of emotions. This reduces stress and gives the freedom to incorporate the attitude of playfulness. It is important to begin to look for the positive in life to start attracting this. Then you can reinvent yourself and joyfully create the life you desire. It is possible to replace regret with joy

When unbalanced self-parenting tapes run over and over, the thoughts keep returning to what has been lost or to what someone has done wrong. It is more constructive to work on building a path to the desired future. The secret of letting something upsetting go is to implement the process of *mindfulness* and to focus on the emotion of joy.

Mindfulness is a process of being consciously aware of your environment and your reactions. A focusing technique is practiced with breathing techniques to monitor one's feelings. By using *mindfulness*, catch yourself in the process of unbalanced self-parenting that involves self-defeating emotional cycles. Replace this pestlet pattern with thoughts and feelings of something that brings Joyful Sprinklet. Write a list of five things that make you feel joyful. Carry this list with you. Share this activity with your children to get them to be focused on their own 'present -moment behavior.'

The thoughts of joy become a comforting way to give yourself a peaceful outlook on the future based on new balanced self-parenting. Combined this with self-esteem building practices. Make a second list of your good qualities. Read this list the first thing each morning and the last thing at night. In a few weeks, you can begin to expectantly feel there is hope of a new beginning. You are actively creating a place in your heart for this possibility by mindful focus on this new life option. Look at the lessons you have learned from your past relationship with yourself and others. Let go of the regret and regained your sense of worth. Teach your children this self-parenting trait to let go the pestlet behaviors of yesterday.

The third part of the new self-parenting reprogram process is to fill your mind with thoughts of those things that bring you gratitude. By holding gratitude as your main emotion, and filling your heart with hopeful anticipation, you can open the door to a new life based on self-love and success. Hopeful Sprinklet and Grateful Sprinklet are your focus.

Loving Your Inner Child

In his book "Acknowledgment of the Inner Child," Dr. Hugh Misslidine teaches that the inner child of the past is formed by the overall environment, rather than one traumatic experience. The child discovers himself or herself by the caretaker's reactions. If there was not supportive early parenting, the void is created for nurturing. This need remains to be filled as an adult to receive gentle guidance, rather than intimidation and judgmental harshness.

Misslidine stresses the key to heal this is to replace this pattern by parenting yourself lovingly with patience. Leave the old behind as you no longer look at yourself through the eyes of others who were in the role of authority figures. Assume this authority within yourself to act as the loving protector to the child within. Provide forgiveness and acceptance of self. Decide that you don't deserve any more punishment for mistakes made. As you heal your own inner child, you begin to parent yourself and your children in more constructive ways.

The sadden child within who has been hurt plays games to protect the wounded ego. Others are not impressed by the arrogant behavior which often results. The insecure individual who has been humiliated as a child puts up masks, avoids intimacy and demonstrates Smug Pestlet behavior. A person either builds bridges or walls in relationships. If the inner child is held trapped in patterns of fear, anger and insecurity, freedom is hindered. This comes by replacing attitudes and past stereotyping with self-supporting nurturing actions.

The child may help construct a sentence that will affirm something he/she is working on like self-image, consistency or behavioral changes. Here are a few suggested affirmations for children to practice auto-suggestions that remind them of the desired behavior:

"I am kind. I am a loving boy (or girl). I put up my toys. I am kind to our pet. I eat my meal. I take a nap. I go to bed on time." When sharing these with a child, select one that is most appropriate and have him/her repeat three times. Make it a game to note ways the child is demonstrating this target behavior. Practice affirmations or examples working with the same target behavior seven times throughout the day for 21 days. Cycles of change have been found in repetitions of twenty-one.

Suggested Affirmations for Constructive Parenting of Self and Others:

Choose one and repeat it 21 times for 21 days:

> — I am calm.
> — I am grateful for small and large blessings in life.
> — I like myself. I love myself.
> — I let go of others to the highest good of all.
> — I set priorities and manage time effectively.
> — I go beyond forgiveness to the lesson learned.
> — I am inner controlled.
> — I persevere to attain those things I desire.
> — I love and accept the child within unconditionally.
> — I promise to take consistent care of this inner child.
> — I claim my rights and stand up for my space.
> — I am kind and supportive to myself and others.

Affirmation Agreement

Write a 21-day agreement to surrender all into pure unconditional love. Journal your progress daily. Affirm: "I let everything go except pure love in my life."

Strength and Integrity

Looking at who you are is looking at all of your qualities - everything- the sprinklets and the pestlets. It is also accepting it all without judgment. It is the way one interprets happenings which causes pain. The ability to be happy depends on how much power one gives the illusion of lack. Your strength is directly related to your greatest fears and anger. Make a list of your fears and anger. Turn them into a healing affirmation in your life.

Thoughts are like drops of water. With our own thoughts, we can become drown in a sea of pestlet energy, or float on an ocean of loving waters. Every thought and word is an affirmation so use self-control to decide what you allow in your experience. The key is to replace negative thoughts with positive ones. Teach your children these concepts in age-appropriate ways.

Joy Therapy

Use positive imagery with calming harmonious music. Fill with unconditional love.

Energy blocks are formed as stress is held in the body. Release these by the use of sound.

Toning was first expressed by Laurel Elizabeth Keys in the early 1970's. She taught to take a deep breath and let out a sound on the exhale. Tone a word on each note of the chromatic scale to releases tension and balance the brain. Tone the vowels. Sighing is another beneficial sound to make to release tension.

Dance in free movement expression. Put on some lively music and dance by yourself. Ask your children to join you in moving to the beat of the music. Children can learn to release inhibition as they get lost in the rhythm of the sound.

Teach your children to support their own 'Inner Child' and to have sprinklet experiences.

The Path of Accomplishment

Live your goal. If life isn't thrilling, make it so. your Make your imagination work for you. Practice handling things the way you choose before they happen. New habits are not formed under stress. Let nothing outside take you off your inner balance. Mentally enact the response you want to incorporate into your behavior pattern before it takes place. What you believe, you become. Practice a positive self-image. Concepts are containers that shape you. Whatever the mind assumes is true will eventually produce itself.

Observation is an effective tool for growth. Observe what you are doing instead of beating yourself up for doing it. Acknowledge small baby steps of progress on life's journey. The best way to undo a wrong is to start loving yourself. Look at intolerable situations constructively. Stand firm and refuse to accept attack. No longer allow yourself to be treated as a collection of someone else's projection. Know your true worth. Teach this approach to living to your children.

A person only puts another down when he/she feels out of control and insecure. The path to happiness is not a straight and narrow road without setbacks or roadblocks. When the going gets tough, the tough get going. Recall the details of a time when you were successful. Bring these feelings into the present. Find courage in a still small place in your heart.

Value Your Self

The stillness within the core of self is who you truly are (not all the glitter of accomplishments, which do, or don't, surround you.) A false value is formed when self-esteem is judged and weighed on those things we can buy, the awards we have accumulated, or what others say about us. If prizes are one's monitoring reference, the individual is vulnerable to the environment and always on a scale of comparison. Self-worth is the foundation of bounty we allow ourselves to attain. If one feels incompetent, weak or undeserving from a low self-image, this is limited and pestlets rule the outcome.

Art Activity to do with your children: Draw a picture of a person; Fill the inside with a description of the person who is your 'Ideal self.' This is who you want to be. Self-love comes as you live closer to this expectation. Discuss ways with your children that they can be the 'Ideal Self' they want to be. Daily find ways to live you can all live in accordance with this. The highest accomplishment is to become your own best friend and protector of the child within yourself.

Set short term realistic goals and acknowledge weekly progress. Even though you may have periods of falling short of this plan, put your dreams into action for long term accomplishment. Get rid of attitudes and actions that don't make you feel peace, pleasure and safety. Make life simple. Teach your children this value!

Being True to One's Self: Recovering You Own Inner Child

Being an effective parent is related to enjoying your own 'Inner Child.' Break a routine so life isn't so predictably boring. Be alert to numbness and non-feeling emotional states. Let the child you are feel excitement of each new day. Draw who you are from your place of power within. Align this with the strength of the will in the balanced, happy child within. This child is flexible and can bend as the willow tree when the winds of time blow. Focus on what it is in yourself which allowed you to survive difficult times in the past. Function from this when challenges come. Take better care of this delightful spontaneous child. Go into the amazing 'World of Sprinklets' every day. Take your children with you.

NLP Time-Line

Set up a NLP Time-line. To do this, pace off an area of ten feet long to represent the life path you have walked until now. Close your eyes and imagine you are walking this with kind people who make the child within feel loved, safe and important. As you walk the time-line journey, let everything go except the loving, affectionate support. Maintain this sense of security and wholeness in the way you live.

Make this an activity to do with a child who is expressing pestlet behavior. Guide them to do a Sprinklet Walk and join you in the World of Sprinklet Power.

A child is unique

Each child's problems are unique

The Solutions will be unique

Self-Parenting Release Imagery

Visualize holding your parent's hand and release them loving to the highest good. No longer be externally dependent by your parent tapes or by your environment. See that you are symbolically putting to rest the negative parts of your past experience. Make a closure on this chapter of life. Pull forth the lessons learned and go on. One is either running from the past or learning from it. A person may find the same type of person as a dysfunctional parent to continue childhood abuse issues. Say goodbye to this phase as you say hello to your life of self-comfort and sprinklet self-parenting skills.

Factors to Recover a Wounded Inner Child

1. Allow yourself to be less than perfect and still be loved. If the child in you doesn't understand this, you won't be able to objectively look at reality and your behavior.
2. Stop taking things personally. Stay out of conflicts regarding who is right or wrong. Examine your reality. You are not necessarily wrong because someone points a finger at you. Be true to yourself. Don't adjust your reality just to fit another's opinion. Don't lose yourself trying to please others. The practice of humility opens avenues to freedom. False pride blocks the way to free expression. Don't become Smug Pestlet.
3. Lighten up in life and add a humorous outlook. Be Joyful Sprinklet in the present moment.

Embracing Your Own Inner Child

— If you stop abandoning yourself, the child within will never be abandoned again. Let go of the fairytale of finding need fulfillment outside yourself; Then you can make dreams come true. This does not mean giving up the luxury of being loved by other people. It means we each take care of our own emotional needs. We enjoy one other, allowing each to be free to be true to himself or herself in the relationship. When you look in the mirror affirm, "I am lovable." Please the person in the mirror. You can't please everyone so be the person you are proud to be. Put life struggles on a mental screen and just observe it objectively.
— To truly embrace this child, we each have within, find happiness in little things as children do. Consider how you spend your time. Write a list of your favorite activities. How often do you do these anymore? Do what is important to you. Do one nice thing for yourself each day as a gift to your inner child within. Teach this to your children and share any of the following activities your family can enjoy:
— Sing at least one peppy, positive song each day. The shower, the car or in nature are good places for this.
— Write down your good sprinklet qualities; read out loud daily.
— Relax with three deep breaths. Become a rag doll as you let go of stress on the exhale.
— Purify with water; Drinking pure water flushes toxins from the body.
— Laugh! Laugh! Laughter lessen the burden.
— Count backwards from ten to one. Visualize blue coming in your heart bringing peace.
— Walk in nature with your inner child. Experience through the wonder of a child.
— Imagine you are a wave. Do free movement to the sound of the ocean to music on tape.
— Close your eyes; relax your face with a gentle touch of your fingertips.

- Imagine you are floating on calm water or drifting downstream as a leaf.
- Look for cloud shapes while lying down outside.
- Do free movement for ten minutes. Twist side to side. Make your arms mover like windmills. Kick your legs as high as you can. (safely)
- Establish firm boundaries. A child still acknowledges self and has these unless he or she has been too intimidated. Learn to say "No."
- Speak from your heart.
- Live in the present moment with no past - no future.
- Rock yourself. Hug yourself.
- Release other people's opinion.
- Draw yourself as a little child. What colors did you use?

    Blue = peaceful   yellow = joyful

    red = angry   black = depressed or bored   green = free spirited

- Erase what you don't want in your life from an imaginary easel with a magic eraser. Draw in your favorite sprinklets. Connect with nature by being outside with appreciation for the beauty around you.

Inner Child Visualizations to Share with Children

Close your eyes and take three deep breaths through the nose, releasing through the mouth gently. Count backwards from ten to one letting go more and more with each count. See yourself as a child surrounded by light. Every part of you is illuminated with light which brings clarity. This brilliance fills your being and radiates out in all directions. You feel you are a beacon shining to welcome others who can see. This light forms an egg shape cocoon around you. In this safe space, sense your fears as being outside this cocoon, yet visible to you. Even though these may be small concerns or large fears, you are perfectly protected from them. Now see the solutions to these situations appear. What action will you take? Open your eyes to a new beginning of empowerment.

Inner Child Imagery

Close your eyes and take three deep breaths as above. Visualize a rainbow arch appearing before you. This spans the sky from where you are now to where you want to be. Step on this bridge of love and light and allow the colors to move into you bringing relaxation. of your being. At the end of this rainbow is the happy child you are within. Embrace this innocent, beautiful one and give the promise to always keep the child safe in presence of loving companionship. Be attentive to this child and allow her/him to be heard. Thank your child for the time spent together and help in any way possible to fulfill any request the child made. As you return over the rainbow, know a part of this child is still in your heart. Open your eyes to the new world.

The Passage-Rite of the Child
Share this with Preteens

The healing of the child involves growing up at all levels physically and psychology. Otherwise the person is operating in the adult world as the same child of the past. He/she is in a grownup body interacting with a group of others with the pressure and responsibility of the adult world.; Yet if this closure has not transpired, the person 's maturation is in an age lock psychologically from the time of trauma. There is a passage rite into womanhood or manhood necessary to move on to heal the inner child and function as an integrated adult.

Passage Rite Ceremony

Get yourself in a comfortable position with your eyes closed. Take three deep breaths through the nose and release through the mouth. Continue relaxed breathing as you begin to visualize yourself when you were a child. Send this child love, understanding and validation. Let the child become filled with this bonding experience. Build trust as you promise to always be present with the child and consider his /her needs. Promise to allow this child to grow and make mistakes in a nurturing, supportive environment which you will provide. Now watch as the child begins to mature and grow into the balanced person that this unconditional love fostered. Allow the child to go through developmental phases necessary. See the child grow and heal into a secure adult. As you acknowledge this closure on childhood, bring forth the qualities this delightful time of life offers. Incorporate the spontaneity, joy, exuberance and playfulness of youth. When the passage into your adult state feels enacted, come back to alert awake awareness.

Parenting the Self with Healthy Communication

Virginia Satir, author of the book "Communication: Talking and Listening" relates,

"Communication is the largest single factor determining what kinds of relationships a person makes with others and what happens to us in the world."

Early learning becomes the foundation for the rest of our lives unless something powerful intercedes. Parenting the self puts an emphasis on the necessity of making another person feel important by listening to them. Parents are given the task to develop empathy and the ability to truly listen. Communication is a learned process in which we use the elements of our bodies, sense organs, brains, expectations, and values.

At times it becomes impossible for someone to get past their preconceived ideas and parent tapes to see the true picture. Sometimes a person is projecting what they themselves are doing or feeling and claiming this behavior is the traits of another person. Stair directs, "Give yourself the luxury of fully looking without talking. Notice body posture, muscles, facial and body nuances and coloring. Do this imagery for one minute and close your eyes.

See how clearly you perceive the other person. Notice the judgments formed. Is there a comparison to yourself? This is part of your internal dialog. Does it make you stiffen, feel dizzy or embarrassed, or does it make you feel good and relaxed? Developing intimacy connects people to the ability to have clear honest communication. When each family member tells what they can about their inner space of attitude, inner self-dialog and parent tapes, it provides a safety zone to resolve trouble in a relationship.

If dissatisfaction continues, the people involved in these interactions begin to resent each other and find faults. Picking at each other and criticism begins to undermine the trust at the core of the friendship. Then each person pulls away and spends less time with one another. They are unaware of their motives and actions. Many people are unaware of their unconscious thoughts and motives (sprinklets and pestlets). Subliminal communication needs to be addresses to incorporate direct communication based on Honesty Sprinklet.

Many things are not put into words that are communicated in body language and attitude inference. Most people don't hear how they really sound, but only how they intend to sound. We react to voice quality and our friendships are affected. Listen to your own tone of voice and note how it is affecting others response. Look at the true communication that is going on from the buried unbalanced parenting tapes. Self-esteem comes from healing the wounded inner child to bring forth the 'Liberated Noble Child'. The goal in all communication is mutual respect. The challenge is to function from Balanced New Parent, Balanced Wise Analyst and the Noble leadership of the Liberated Child. The question is who and what you will allow in your life? Will you take the power to respond productively, or react unconsciously?

Chapter Eight: Suggestions to Improve Your Family's Health

Integrative Health approach involves several life-style changes, as well as the attitude alterations and self-parenting skills. Coping techniques address mind-body-spiritual imbalances by providing a variety of creative problem-solving tools that involve all the senses. These coping techniques address prioritizing, simplifying and subtracting activities to improve overall health. These also bring greater productivity and implement positive psychology. One's self-image underlies behavior and the attitude to deal with daily stress. The insecurity that underlies becoming overextended results in the need to prove oneself and causes rushing and disorganized behaviors. This pattern can start in early childhood.

Write down your 'To Do List' for the day. Subtract at least three things that are not priorities.

Write a list of the scheduled activities your child has each week. This may include sports, dance and music lessons. Add in time for study and chores. Add in unstructured time for leisure activities. Address how much time is spent in internet activities with the phone and computer. Limit this to a restricted amount daily and increase time in nature. Children's time is overscheduled by school functions, sports, extra-curricular activities and media interests. A calm state of mind is the basis of a peaceful home and congenial relations. Kindness Sprinklet is the leader of respect within the family and replaces self -destructive behaviors that can lead to mental and emotional issues.

Importance of Diet and Exercise on Mental and Emotional Balance

Dr. Dean Ornish, MD, author of "The Spectrum," recommends the *Rainbow Diet* to eat a variety of rich vibrant colored foods and a variety of textures and flavors to provide fuel for your cells. Make eating a ritual. Eat more slowly and chew thoroughly because digestion starts in the mouth with saliva.

Sugar is connected to hyperactivity, candida and digestive and immune disorders. It causes bone loss and tooth decay. High fructose corn syrup is concentrated sugar. Avoid sodas, including diet soda. Drink 2/3 oz. purified spring water per pound of body weight daily.

Nuts are good snacks (unless there is an allergy). Organic fresh fruit, nuts or raw vegetables with nut butter is recommended for snacks.

Eat fruit on an empty stomach. These are good sources of antioxidants and flavonoids which enhance the activity of vitamin C for immunity. Organic strawberry is the best source of these nutrients. All fruits and vegetables need to be organic. Kiwi is a good source of potassium, magnesium, vitamin E and fiber. It has twice the vitamin C as an orange. Watermelon is a key source of lycopene, vitamin C and potassium. Avoid all preservatives, fertilizers, hormones and chemical additivities in food.

Eat small amounts of lean red meat, fowl, eggs and unlimited organic green vegetables and fish. The astaxanthin in skin of salmon fight free radicals which damage cell membranes.

Don't combine eating fruit and protein for best digestion. Eat non-starchy vegetables with grains (This includes, broccoli, spinach, cabbage, cauliflower, celery, carrots and sprouts).

Organic avocado, safflower, sesame, sunflower and olive oil are the best unsaturated oils. Leafy greens contain lutein which protects against system inflammation.

Eat gluten free bread and pasta in small amounts only. Avoid all caffeine (including chocolate). Use low sodium foods and do not add salt at the table or when cooking. Read labels for salt, carbohydrate and sugar content, as well as preservatives and additives Cow's milk has casein which is a glue-like substance causing asthma, mucus and brain congestion. Research has identified a milk protein as a possible cause of attention deficit disorder. Almond milk, cashew and coconut milk and rice milk are much healthier options and are easier to digest.

Exercise is one of the best things to do for your health of body and mind. Exercise reduces behavioral problems and obesity and normalizes hormones. It makes you more efficient and can even help grow new brain cells through a process called neurogenesis. To address stress, exercise at least 30 minutes in the morning. Get out in the sun. Walking in the evening promotes restful sleep and clearing of the mind. Exercise reduces the effects of the stress hormone cortisol. Stress is a factor in digesting food and assimilating nutrients for optimal brain and organ function.

Another author on diet and healthy living is Steven R. Gundry, MD. He has written the book entitled "The Plant Paradox." It gives a quick and easy 30- day plan to feel great and live lectin free. His meal plans for families and recipes offer a complete tool kit for health benefits.

Benefits of Purified Spring Water

Pure water is vital for energy production in the cells for overall metabolism and neurotransmitters. The treatment of the whole body is the path to full system efficiency.

Water removes free radicals from the body and brain.

Purified water aids strong bone formation.

Pure water improves the efficiency of the immune system to combat infections.

Pure water is needed for the production melatonin to regulate healthy sleep patterns.

Don't drink water or cook with water from a home with a water softener. (It adds sodium

Water is a conductor of energy. Even mild dehydration affects the vitality level and lethargy that relates to mood disorders, emotional control and exhaustion. Dehydration can be a precursor to emotional and mental disorders. Emotions are synthesized and harmonize by purified or spring water.

Detrimental Effects of Stress on Body and Brain Function

Stress is your body's response to certain situations. Stress is subjective; something that may be stressful for one person may not be stressful for someone else. Not all stresses are bad; for example, graduating from college may be considered a 'good' stress. Stress can affect your physical health, your mental health, and your behavior. In response to stressful stimuli, your body turns on its biological response: chemicals and hormones are released that are meant to help your body rise to the challenge.

Your heart rate increases, your brain works faster and becomes razor sharp, you have a sudden burst of energy. This response is natural and basic; it's what kept our ancestors from falling victim to hungry predators. Stress overload, however, can have harmful effects. We cannot eliminate stress from our lives, but we can learn to avoid and manage it.

When a person is stressed, all body systems begin to become unable to function optimally; if this continues, eventually chronic stress causes breakdown and crisis. Relaxation techniques are effective coping skills to intercede in this because they affect physical, mental and spiritual. Tension causes the release of stress hormone, cortisol, and other harmful hormones that can cause reduction in brain synapsing and acuity. The stress hormone reduces the ability to reason rationally and affects long term memory and concentration. These same repercussions are present physically, emotionally and mentally when a child is under stress.

Coping Techniques for Stress

Improving sleep patterns is one of the best ways to reduce stress and optimize brain and emotional control. What you eat and think affects your ability to sleep. Avoid eating pasta and meat casserole late in the evening. Carbohydrates, as well as sugary desserts can cause moodiness and a racing mind. Poor digestion can be related to getting less sleep. Catnip/lemon balm tea and taking one tablespoon of apple cider vinegar with honey or Aloe herbal Juice for indigestion. Avoid carbonated sodas also. The sugar substitutes in diet drinks can wire the nervous system just as sugar and caffeine do. Chamomile herb tea at bedtime can calm the nervous system. The herb Lobelia can help normalize emotional balance, strengthen the glandular system and build immunity and stamina. All these suggestions are relevant for brain development in children and in brain function.

Caffeine in coffee, sodas and chocolate can accelerate the nervous responses and over stimulate heart and nerves. Teccino Mediterranean Herbal Coffee Alternative is made from roasted almonds, dates and figs. Replace the caffeine with fresh fruits, fish and organic vegetables. This improved nutrition can give the body a reservoir of vitamins and minerals to better deal with the stress and to be more centered within. The detoxing process may cause you to feel tired for a few days, but soon you should enjoy more vitality and a sunnier disposition than you have in years. This detoxing effect can clear mental fog in those of all ages.

Cleansing toxicity is a factor in getting enough restful sleep to rejuvenate the body. Drinking at least eight to ten or more 8 oz. of purified room temperature water during the day is vital in getting a good night's sleep. Double your intake of purified room temperature water for three days with sage tea and senna tea while eating only organic fruits, vegetables and leafy greens. Following this cleanse, stabilize your diet with plentiful servings of leafy greens for regularity. Eat meat and eggs from animals raised in grass feed healthy environments without hormones and pesticides. It is best to eat these in moderation with smaller serving.

The is a suggested plan for body/mind detox to bring the system into acid alkaline balance. This program included drinking six (8 oz.) glasses of purified water with a slice of fresh lemon, three cups of Milk Thistle Herbal Tea and three cups of Dandelion Herbal Tea daily. Followed this plan and eat mainly a diet of organic vegetables and fruits for twenty-one days to cleanse the colon and give his digestive system a rest.

Integrative Mind/Body Process to Maintain a Healthy Lifestyle

Creative problem solving involves whole brain function. The left-brain analytical skill is accessed, as well as the right brain incubating technique. Abstract and concrete are brought to bear to facilitate more effective resolutions. Gestalt is an effective form of problem solving through the physical release of turning emotions outward rather than suppressing them. In this technique, individuals can use physical activity to move the energy of their repressed feelings.

Practice the Following to Release Anger and Pent-up Emotions:

Physical exercise	Breath Imageries
Singing/music/chanting	Journaling (especially effective for teens)
Rapid walking	Leisurely walking to connect with nature

Ways to Build a Child's Self-Confidence

In her book "Creative Conflict Resolution," Kristen Simmons gives an excellent summary of ways to build or destroy self-confidence:

- Help them develop their natural interests and skill.
- Help them succeed in school.
- Break difficult tasks into manageable parts.
- Allow for mistakes and encourage perseverance.
- Help children set realistic goals.
- Give honest and specific praise based on actual accomplishments often.
- Expect them to help out in the home and in the community.
- Let them know how much you love them regularly.

Ways to Reduce A Child's Self-Confidence

Dwelling on trivial experiences

Sarcasm and criticizing while talking down to them

Never admitting you are wrong

Giving threatening orders

Doing most of the talking and little listening

Bringing up past mistakes

Emotional Health: Attitude Adjustment for Behavior Changes

Destructive pestlet emotions such as unforgiveness, fear of failure and anger cause biochemical changes in the brain. Forgiveness is a coping technique that allows an individual carrying a grudge to take personal care of him/herself by letting go of emotions that can cause biochemical and hormonal changes. These result in unstable conditions emotionally and physically. It is not necessary to discuss this with the offending person for the process to free this emotional holding pattern.

It is important to come to the awareness that even if the anger or resentment is justified, it is not worth the destructive effects it is creating in reducing the vitality and joy of living in the person carrying the emotion. Journaling and letter writing are effective modes of catharsis. The letters may be too caustic to mail and need to be torn up to represent the end of accepting this kind of treatment. They need to be rewritten until the letter can express the sprinklet love. underneath all pain, anger, fear and other pestlets. Art Therapy can be effective for a child to express what he or she cannot put in written words.

Three Places Where Anger Lives

The past - Dwelling on and reacting to what is already over:

When an angry thought comes to the surface of your mind. Recognize it and let it float on by. If you grab it and mull it over, it diminishes alert capacities of present moment mindful concentration. This happening that made you mad is over so there is nothing you can do about it except dwell on it. By doing this you inflict self-destruction and draw negativity to yourself.

Affirm: "The past cannot touch me or take away my happiness."

The Present - Reaction to something that is happening right now:

You can control this by taking positive self-supportive action. Discuss possible solutions with an authority or mentoring source to determine the best action to take. The mind reaches clarity through use of right brain creativity and left/brain logic of whole brain function to reach solutions. Affirm:" I take care of my needs with loving concern and resolution."

The Future – Reacting to something that hasn't happened:

Dwelling on thoughts of the future of things that might happen is based on speculation and worry. Worry takes you into imagined events that may not even happen. If the event comes to pass, you can handle it constructively with clear logic and creativity. This is much more effective than being distracted by a fear-based illusion and negativity that draws self-defeating outcomes. Affirming solutions are available opens the mind to receive these insights.

Affirm: "I know the best action to resolve this issue."

By using coping skills, a three-fold process of self-discovery emerges: severance from old ways and reaching a threshold through an internal inventory that reveals creative solutions and guidance in a transition period. This leads to incorporation of the new insights to progress personal development and reduce the impact of stressors.

When a person believes harmful criticism, the process of cause and effect can become a self-fulfilling prophecy and limit possibilities. Example of formative proclamation: "I can't do anything right." This creates patterns of destructive thoughts and consequences. Positive thinking advocates and scientists have proven the creative power of thoughts and words. Stress patterns from the pestlet emotions which follow pestlet thinking, result in biochemical changes that are destructive to the brain, as well as every gland and organ in the body.

In an escalating process of decline, blood pressure becomes elevated, cells become toxic and the immune system breaks down. Positive affirmations can redirect this process to work on one's behalf. Instead of living as the stress-filled victim, an individual can begin to foster joy and stabilize emotional balance.

A pattern of low self-esteem that fosters negativity, frustration and powerlessness causes defensiveness and blaming others for weaknesses. It is important to recognize environmental influences that foster expressions of a narrow range of emotions. Denial of one's emotions restricts the expression of them.

Your Emotions and You: Who is in Charge?

Anger is often ignored, avoided or suppressed causing emotion/related health issues. Until anger is recognized, it cannot be expressed correctly. Depression is generally recognized as repressed anger. A sense of being out of control of one's environment can cause a deep level of buried anger. Many times, when this is acknowledged, and steps are taken to gain better communication and compromise, the anger subsides, as well as the depression. Studies have shown that physical exercise results in a less depressed state of mind.

Emotional well-being is the ability to feel and express the entire range of human emotions, and to control them, not be controlled by them. Emotions have begun to be a focus of research relating hormonal output from stress to the breakdown of physical and mental functions. Balanced Integrative Health can only be accomplished by monitoring one's emotions and redirecting them.

The 'parent tapes' hold the key to access hot buttons and stress causing factors and fears. Many health problems are thought to be directly tied to our inability to constructively vent feelings. This builds up the level of the stress hormone cortisol which has clinically proven to trigger hormonal imbalances and plaque "tangles" of bad protein in brain cells. These are for-runners to memory loss. Relaxation, balance of work, play and rest are self-care processes that support longevity. It is important to learn ways to take personal responsibility for one's reactions.

The ultimate responsibility lies within each person Responsibility for our well-being begins with the thoughts we think, the foods that we eat and the environment we allow to cause us stress and worry. It begins in prevention and personal care for our quality of life and choices of personal balanced parenting. A healthy lifestyle is a whole-body process of accountability with honesty in our interactions, intake of pure water, food and focus on the positive. Balance in health can only take place when there is harmony in mental, physical, emotional and spiritual levels. De-toxing gives life meaning and the vitality to enjoy the moment. If the unconscious mind has victim patterns and false beliefs about our worth, these erroneous attitudes impede our chosen goals.

Use mindfulness to focus on what you are doing and thinking. This can replace harmful self-talk and aid in creating a healthy lifestyle. The things we think about and claim with our words tend to become our reality. If pain, rushing and overload dominate our days, we lose precious time that could be spent in laughter, joy and anticipation of exciting adventures.

Technique to Clear the Mind

Get comfortable and play calm music. Close your eyes. Inhale and exhale to the count of five. Repeat five times.

Imagine you are in a place where you are relaxed and happy. Imagine this in detail. See yourself in the center of you own heart where unconditional love connects to all life. Now visualize you are on a meadow in clean air and sunshine.

Imagine you are floating leisurely on still water.

Imagine you are in a clearing of a beautiful forest.

Experience this renewal and calm.

Count from one to five. Move your fingers and toes as you return to the ever vibrant 'now.'

Giving Life New Meaning by Introspecting Your Choices

When a person believes a harmful saying, the process of cause and effect can become a self-fulfilling prophecy and limit possibilities. Examples of formative proclamation are the sayings "I can't do anything right." This creates patterns of destructive thoughts and consequences. Positive affirmations can redirect this process to work on one's behalf. Instead of living as the stress-filled victim, an individual can begin to foster joy and stabilize emotional balance with sprinklets.

A pattern of low self-esteem that fosters negativity, frustration and powerlessness causes defensiveness and blaming others for weaknesses. It is important to recognize environmental influences that foster expressions of a narrow range of emotions. Denial of one's emotions restricts the expression of them and causes a numbing effect. Experiencing one's good qualities builds a positive self-concept and enables the person to accept their full range of emotions. This reduces stress and gives the freedom to incorporate the attitude of playfulness. It is important to begin to look for the positive in life to start attracting this. Then you can create the life you desire with focused attention on remedial exercises and goal setting.

The people that make it in this world look around for the circumstance they want, and if they don't find it, they create it. Most of one's sense of struggle and anxiety stems from an overactive mind. If you take your goals too seriously, you forget to have fun along the way.

Live a life filled with love. Compassion is a heartfelt emotion that delivers kindness to everyone we meet. Listen! Listen! Listen! You have two ears and one mouth so talk half as much as you listen. Don't make others feel they are competing with you for 'airtime' in a conversation. Notice if you are the only getting a chance to talk. Allow yourself downtime. We have become 'human doings' instead of 'human beings.' The beauty of doing nothing allows you to clear your mind and relax in the flow of creativity.

Chapter Nine: Creating the Better Self

Core Issue: The person's thoughts and attitudes have a direct effect on their feelings. These either come from the balanced or the unbalanced parenting influences that are permitted to continue. The influences are generated from within and from interactions with others. These attitudes come from concepts and phrases that form the framework of the belief system. The power to change the words that anchor unbalanced programming is within and is activated by a choice to change these and become their 'Better Self.".

In his book "Escaping the Labyrinth," David W. Sohn states,

"Change is created from getting so unhappy with things as they are, we will do what it takes to make them improve. Accepting the fact that we can change is the premise of co-creating new actions to reinvent ourselves. If we are going to have different results, we have to stop doing the same things over and over. We must place our focus on self-control and personal growth, rather than trying to change someone else. We must become inner directed and align the conscious and unconscious mind by introspection. To *medicate* means to heal by giving control to outside influences, while *meditate* means to heal from within."

Many people are locked into a crisis state of frantic thoughts that invade their inner peace. These repetitive thought patterns have become habitual. Sohn recommends affirmations to create clarity and let go of harmful attitudes and beliefs surrounding an issue or relationship:

Repeat these affirmations aloud three times to let go of judgement, struggle and guilt:

"I love myself. Life flows easily for me."

"There is enough love and money for all I desire."

Write these three bolded affirmations one at time and wait briefly for your unconscious mind to respond. Note the brain's first impressions and responses that are elicited. With each resisting thought, firmly say the word 'Cancel.' Affirm "I am rejecting all false beliefs which don't support my prosperity". Visualize a flow of pure crystalline liquid pouring through your cells cleansing away the old unbalanced parenting memory base of illusions. This establishes new self-parenting habit patterns.

Coping Techniques

Reframing your attitude is a prioritizing technique that helps minimize stress and help in organizational skills. This involves taking another look at a situation from a new perspective. Creating new frameworks gives freedom from dysfunctional emotions of guilt, fear and anger that can immobilize progressive action. Reframing techniques can involve not only making a change of attitude, but also by letting go of stereotyping and upsetting concepts. By reframing patterns of unbalanced parenting from childhood, a new internal language is created in the unconscious mind. The memory base is directed through mindfulness and focused thoughts to form a new reality on balanced parenting tapes. This is accomplished by going into a light state of self-hypnosis and creating another reality of a past event visualizing a more harmonious outcome using Neuro Linguistic Programming (NLP).

Another very effective coping technique to restructure unbalanced parent tapes is art therapy. This involves drawing a picture to represent a metaphor of a feeling or life event. This can also be a picture of a familiar house, a relationship, or a time in life. This creative process utilizes the language of the unconscious mind which express in colors, symbols and abstracts.

Simply drawing abstracts, color blends, or child-like representations can bring emotions and memories to the surface when the person has unconsciously integrated them and is ready to release the experience. Some repressed memories in the feeling levels of grief, sadness, anger and fear are too disruptive to be defined in words. The art abstracts that are drawn with a specific intent to heal a relationship can be extremely informative and helpful.

Creative problem solving involves whole brain function. The left-brain analytical skill is accessed, as well as the right brain incubating technique. Abstract and concrete are brought to bear to facilitate more effective resolutions. Writing with your alternate hand can trigger a new perspective from another angle through word and letter formation in writing.

Forgiveness is a coping technique that allows an individual carrying a grudge to take personal care of himself by letting go of emotions that can cause biochemical and hormonal changes which can make him or her sick emotionally and physically. It is not necessary to discuss this with the offending person for the process to free this emotional 'holding pattern.' It is important to come to the awareness that even if the anger or resentment is justified, it is not worth the destructive effects it is creating in reducing the vitality and joy of living in the person carrying the emotion.

Journaling your thoughts and feelings is effective modes of catharsis. Journaling after meditation to record a vision quest brings a person into deep levels of healing introspection. Another technique is to journal names of people you resent, why and how long you have felt this way. Ask yourself if this is productive. This can not only bring forgiveness, but also provide creative problem solving.

Gestalt is another effective form of problem solving through the physical release of emotions with physical movement, rather than suppressing them. Beat a pillow or scream to get the energy moving that has held the unbalanced parent programming in the bondage of tortured thoughts and feelings. Exercise and expressive dance are tools to move energy and thus release blocked emotions. Movement is another path to forgiveness.

During the implementation of these coping techniques a person triggers a time of self-discovery which brings *incorporation* of the new insights based on the balanced parenting process of the *Wise Analyst*.

Build a Balanced Life: Avoid the Stress of Overload

Building the basis of a balanced life involves avoiding overload by setting up a schedule that includes time for rest, sleep, work and recreation. Learn to say no to some of the demands on the various life roles. Establishing healthy boundaries is critical in starting to take better care of yourself. "Practicing the Art of Subtraction" by Brain Luke Seaward, involves learning to prioritize and to incorporate activities that are self-nurturing. Find ways to use time more efficiently by implementing new organizational techniques. Write "To Do List" highlighting the ten most important things to do. Start delegating some of the errands and household chores when possible. Work together as a team with other household members to divide the necessary work.

A low self-image can factor into the choices that are made on how to use time each day. As a greater priority is placed on nurturing yourself, some of the new choices involve time to sit and absorb the beauty and fresh air outside. A short brisk walk combined with about fifteen minutes to linger in calm sites allows you to clear your mind, relax and get better sleep.

Become aware of your thoughts so that you can be more patient with yourself and your personal expectations. The self-driven patterns of perfectionism began to diminish you began use balanced parenting to love and respect yourself in more ways. When old pestlet, judgmental thoughts show up, replace them with a focus on your good qualities. Make a list of these and review this daily to take care of your own needs, as well as the needs of others. Let go of critical unbalanced messages to yourself that drain vitality and create emotions of guilt.

Self-love is a gift you give yourself and those you love. Taking care of yourself is one of the best ways to take care of others so you do not become a burden on them. Quality time spent as a family begins to create a bond that brings peace and joy. Tension levels reduce as you enjoy life fully even though you still have a busy schedule.

High stress levels and chronic negative attitudes can create biochemical changes from that cause toxic conditions throughout his organs and glands. A stressed personality contributes to general toxicity. The stress of low self-esteem is based in unbalanced parenting behaviors:

One of the core behaviors of the insecure personality is fear of getting close to anyone. Self-pity stems from feelings of being unloved and isolated. Stress and loneliness accelerate traits of perfectionism. Affirmations are helpful to reprogram early unbalanced parenting. These are positive statements that redirect the unconscious mind to align with specific message to release buried emotions and attitudes that are counter to this. These affirmations reorient the attitude to strengthen self-concept: "I love and approve of myself."

"I express my feelings openly and am patient with myself."

"I am qualified to do a good job and finish what I start."

Get in Touch with Your Own Body and Energy Systems

Electromagnetic fields surround the body. Author, Mieka Knaster relates energy sense in her book "Discovering the Body's Wisdom." She relates the body lets you know through your physical symptoms when and where there is trouble. Listen to your body's signals of trauma and emotional duress. Be more aware of your own inner knowing to feel what is transpiring in your own body systems. You need this same awareness of sensitivity to accurately deal with your relationships with others.

The teachings of energy systems are ancient in cultures around the world. This work has advanced greatly in America since Bough Joy, MD, a western medicine pioneer discovered and researched the energy fields from his patient's in the early 1970's. The world holds many miracles awaiting us if we are open minded to consider new possibilities. Energy frequencies of sound provide a means of moving old patterns of repressed emotions from unbalanced parenting. As energy that was involved in holding down buried emotions is freed, more energy is available. The following activities bring balance to all the body system for optimum health of the individual. These activities are enjoyable for the family to share.

Use music and movement to bring more vitality with the following music exercises:

Brain Centering Body Movement

(Breathe deeply on each exercise to cleanse lungs and energize your body)

Stand up straight. Bend over like a rag doll and swing back and forth.

Return to standing, raising slowly as though you are unfolding one vertebra at a time.

Focus on your posture by sending energy through the soles of your feet to get balanced.

Imagine you are a tree with roots growing into the ground with branches reaching to the sky.

Shoulder Lifts - Inhale deeply as you lift - hold - exhale as shoulders drop 5x's

Shoulder Rolls - 5x's backward and 5x's forward – as you breathe deeply

Arm rolls - 5x's backward and 5x's forward - as you breathe deeply

Windmills - 5x's backward and 5x's forward - as you breathe deeply

Arm Cross - crisscross arms and then swing arms back, opening chest 5x's

Sky Stretch – Reach for the sky with alternate hands 5x's each hand

Head Twist – Slowly roll once to each side, looking over your shoulder

Gentle neck roll – clockwise and counterclockwise - 1x each

Windmill/Torso Twist – exhale bending down – inhale coming back up

Stretch legs and calf by stepping out to the front and side alternately as far as possible and hold.

Music and Movement

Put on some flowing mood music with wind instruments; slow your breathing, inhaling and exhaling gently to relax to the rhythm of the music.

Then put on some lively music and tap yourself with your fingertips repetitively all over your body especially on her thymus and on the soles of your feet.

Put on some marching music and join in marching to the lively beat. March- Step higher with legs together - step out to the side and step back together. Reach your arms around your chest to give yourselves a hug and rock back and forth.

Use Your Breath to Change Chaos to Inner Calm

No matter what age a person is everyone has an inner environment, as well as the external conditions that go on around us. By controlling our reactions, we stabilized ourselves within. By using mental imagery and breath to control our feelings and reactions to the outer world, we are no longer a ship lost at sea tossed around by the waves of our everyday experiences. Children need these skills as well as their parents. Hyperactivity and heart health need to be addressed at very young ages. Practice visualization of a peaceful scene to counter worry patterns and reacting to the problems of others.

Here is a breathing technique to alter the physical stress which include rapid heartbeat and tension in the muscles and nervous system:

Affirm: "I am breathing in fresh air to increase my energy and relax my body and mind. Inhale slowly to the count of five visualizing the color of sky blue filling your cells with peace. This breath represents changing from being outer directed to being inner directed." As you exhale to the count of five, let go of all the accumulated tension from the events you have felt you had no control over. Repeat five times, each time letting go of lavers of stress.

The Importance of Restful Sleep

Many insomnias are lacking in certain vitamins and minerals including Calcium-magnesium, or B vitamin deficiency, or too high copper levels. Vitamin E deficiency can cause restless leg syndrome. Taking a good organic multi-vitamin/multi-mineral supplement is important since most typical diets are lacking magnesium other nutrients. These levels can be checked by your doctor in a blood test. Start the appropriate supplements that are indicated. Side effects from drugs, can cause loss of sleep, so have your doctor also review any prescriptions. Ritalin use in children has shown heart damage in some cases.

Practice visualization of a peaceful scene to counter worry patterns and reacting to the problems of others. Take a hot Epsom Salt bath with baking soda at bedtime for stress relief. The mindfulness techniques of Jon Kabot-Zinn, author of "Catastrophe Living," are an excellent aid to stress reduction and improved sleep. What you think is a factor in calming yourself. Self-hypnosis and Neuro Linguistic Programming (NLP) are also excellent aids.

The Sleep Breath and Other Tips

Use this Sleep Breath to reach a state of calm: Inhale to the count of five. Exhale to the count of seven and gently puff at the end of each this rhythmic breathing cycle. Continue until you drift off in a restful sleep.

Paul McKenna has written an impressive book called, "I Can Make You Sleep." He gives techniques to overcome the disruption of waking in the night and how to sleep when you want and awaken full of energy. He explains health sleep cycles and how to get them. His research includes the stress of parenting and getting restorative sleep and includes a bedtime CD.

The Sleep Breath: Suggestions for Optimizing Your Sleep

Use this Sleep Breath to reach a state of calm: Inhale to the count of five. Exhale to count of seven and gently puff at the end of each breath. Continue until you drift off to sleep.

Loss of sleep is probably the most underrated problem with health around the world for those of all ages It affects family relations and maturity. Sleep is important for healthy function of all the body systems. It is required to form brain pathways for memory and creativity. These planetary changes in instability of leadership have created a time of integration of unbalanced parenting and repressed trauma. The endocrine system secretes human growth hormones (HGH), a body chemical that stimulates the growth of muscle and tissue during sleep. The body goes into *anabolic states* and conserves energy during sleep as opposed to the *catabolism states* of excessive usage of oxygen needed to conduct daily activities. The cells produce cytokines in sleep to build the immune system. Sleeps helps body cells grow and regenerate.

There are several biological factors that take place as you fall asleep. Your body's natural biological (circadian) rhythms dictate a lowering of your body temperature and alert function so you can go to sleep. Having a light in the room can alter your natural rhythms and interfere with this. Not getting sleep disrupts blood sugar and insulin levels and is a factor in diabetes. Sleep deprivation is a serious problem with many symptoms: Itchy eyes, irritability, depression, anxiety, decreased cognitive function, decreased motor skills and eye/ hand coordination, weight gain and impaired immune system. Lack of sleep causes lowered resistance, and causes faulty thinking, slowed reaction time, more risk taking, and increase of heart disease. Beta-blockers and low progesterone can disrupt sleep.

Sleep problems can be side effects of digestive disorders, allergies, infections, pain, RLS (restless leg syndrome), diabetes, Parkinson's, Alzheimer's, ulcers, headaches, asthma, SAD (Seasonal Affective Disorder), emotional conflict, depression and arthritis. What you eat affects your ability to sleep. Avoid eating pasta and meat casserole late in the evening. Carbohydrates and protein, as well as sugary desserts can disturb restful sleep. Sugar products can be related to moodiness and a racing mind. Poor digestion can be related to getting less sleep. Catnip/lemon balm tea and taking one tablespoon of apple cider vinegar with honey or Aloe Vera Juice for indigestion and acid reflex can also provide an undisturbed night of sleep.

Clearing Breath

Hold the intention of CLEARING in this three-part breath cycle to clear your mind and emotions. Take a deep breath through the nose expanding your belly; exhale slowly through the mouth while sucking in your belly. Visualize you are breathing in the color white.

Inhale to the count of four and exhale to the count of four. Visualize you are breathing the color *white* for purification. Hold the intention of emptying the mind of stagnant thoughts and the lungs of stagnant air. Let go of any turmoil or scattered thoughts.

Hold the intention of emptying all the stress from your body, mind and emotions and filling with peace. Count backwards from ten to one; as you relax. Let your breath gently take you deeper and deeper into your *Heart Center.*

Begin your normal breathing pattern with a focus on listening to the sounds around you. Hold the intention to be aware of yourself fully in the present moment and to continue this in your daily life activities. Count from one to five to return to alert awareness. 1…..2….3….4…..5. Move your fingers and toes as you return to the ever vibrant "Now". Affirm: "I am vibrant and full of vitality".

Being Breath

You can use a breathing technique in the first step called an 'Alternate Being Breath.' Inhale through your nose to the count of five. Hold to the count of five and exhale through the mouth to the count of five. Be with yourself. Be aware of all your organs and thank them for their functions. Dialog with each of them asking ways you can set up; a lifestyle to help them be healthier.

Color Breathing to Change Your Brain

Meditation is a form of controlled contemplation on a single image or peaceful scene or quality. This replaces the endless stream of thoughts and head noise. Breathing techniques are a way of directing one's mind to effectively balance a person's body processes to feel calm and focused in the present moment. Combining breath and color imagery is very effective. This can be done as a singular discipline or during chanting and toning. These processes facilitate one to be more aware and attuned to inner directives. The benefits of deep breathing include alert reasoning, increased stamina, enhanced energy and improved quality of oxygen in the blood. It stimulates growth of new tissue, builds the immune system and lifts the emotions. Breath is the bridge to between the conscious and unconscious mind where the unbalanced parent tapes are stored. Connecting to the elements and to nature is the most effective way to access deep levels of individual conscious as a part of the whole in balance.

Establish a Plan for New Possibilities

1. The Art of Subtraction (Take things out of your life to find the time for what and who you feel is most important).
2. Practice the power of saying "NO" to balance of work, play and rest.
3. Use imagery to implement a new plan of action
4. After taking three balancing breaths at bedtime affirm that when you awaken in the morning you will know the solution to a specific problem. As you drift off to sleep, see this problem being washed away by the ocean. Upon arising, let the tide bring solutions.

Build Better Habits: Five Month Plan for Change in the Family

First Month: Changing a destructive behavioral habit: First Week: To become more aware of the behavior you choose to stop, simply monitor it for one week. Set up a replacement behavior. Do not try to change the behavior at this time. Just practice telling yourself you are replacing this action with the one you have chosen.

Next Three Weeks: List three target behaviors you want to increase daily. Write these three behaviors daily during the next 21 days and practice doing them in your mind as you list them one by one. Set up a reward list. For each time you repeat the desired behavior, reward yourself. (These can be free rewards if your budget doesn't currently allow for extra expenditures.)

Second Month: This whole month concentrate on finishing what you start.

Third Month: This whole month, be truthful (counting white lies too).

Fourth Month: This whole month concentrate on being kind (to yourself as well as others.)

Fifth Month: Practice improving your new chosen behaviors

Follow this new plan step by step. It is not possible to get from the bottom step of the stairs to the top in one leap. It is accomplished in small steps. Keep affirming aloud, "I am patient as I go thru this process of growth and forward motion." Avoid getting angry with yourself if you fall back or don't go forward as fast as you would like.

Build a New Habit

Practice the skill of 'present moment consciousness'

Savor your experiences

Make the most of the time life has given you

Chapter Ten: The Respect Method of Cooperative Discipline

Cooperation in discipline is accomplished only when adults and children work as a team. The key is praise rather than punishment. Directing harsh, angry words and physical pain at the child is a determent to training. Inappropriate behavior needs to be corrected with reminders and restriction. Verbal put downs and nagging are not only unnecessary, they are extremely destructive. The home environment is the most critical factor in the increase in violence. Speak in a firm tone, rather than yelling orders of immediate obedience to accelerate defiance.

Make requests which are within the child's comprehension level. Break down each activity into digestible parts. Give fast chances for correction of the offense. Encourage progress of effort applied. Cease to criticize and verbally berate the child about being a terrible mess who never does anything right. Even if the adult doesn't go to this extreme, damage can be done to the child fragile and forming self-concept. If you want to teach a child to admit their mistakes, learn from them and go on, you must adopt two strategic actions. First, think in terms of small consequences to repair the situation. Don't make a big deal out of every misbehavior.

In studies of psychologist Alfred Alder, from 1870 to 1937, he concluded that respect of self is directly related to respect from others. Case studies attested that a confident person behaves more constructively than an insecure individual who has been humiliated. He also proved behavior is motivated by encouragement. Criticism and angry interactions of condemnation thwart emotional growth and maturity. Hope, rather than hostility and hysteria, provides an opportunity for the child to develop independence. Be predictable in your training.

Allow the child to experience the consequence of his/her choices. For example: "You can refuse to do your chore, but you will not leave the house until it is done today." Do not carry restriction past the end of the same day. Let each new morning be another opportunity for a fresh start. Be friends and be an authority figure worth respecting because you live by your words and rules. The purpose of discipline is not to cajole or control, but to bring the person to a place of understanding so that the rights of self and others are respected. Each person, whether big or little in size, has a happy child self within. Adults can more effectively communicate to gain cooperation with young people through this part of themselves.

Self-Reliance and Self-Image

Self-reliance cannot be taught by constant external control. The purpose of discipline is to help the child learn to become independent and maintain functional, appropriate behavior. To develop self-reliant living skills, responsibility is to be given in measured amounts. If the child does not carry out the instructions, he/she has a favorite privilege removed. The concept is that rewards and freedom come in direct proportion to responsibility assumed in life. This is the way the "real adult world" functions. Example: If the child doesn't do his/her homework, TV or another privilege is lost for the night.

A positive self-image is necessary to be secure enough to become independent. The way a person handles his/her angry emotions is a factor in a good self-image. Training a child to handle anger is accomplished by mirroring the adult's pattern in this process. A person can only be in balance when inner control is maintained. Don't allow others to take your control.

Children are mimic the actions of their role models. The child watches an adult lose control and repeats this unhealthy response. Self-respect is not fostered. If the child is allowed to use control mechanisms, no one is going to be in a space of inner control or self-love. These are dawdling, ignoring requests, procrastinating, arguing, talking back and acting incompetent. The following technique is effective in teaching emotional control and self-respect: If the child is using inconsiderate behavior, have him/her write or tape record the appropriate action ten times to learn a better way to handle situations. These are to fit the occasion such as "I speak kindly; I respect others; I do my work neatly and on time; I clean up my own messes." If this is followed through consistently, children use this same reminder to learn better ways of dealing with responses. A cooperative effort is established to work on self-growth. This builds respect and creates more harmonious interactions. The child begins to feel positive as negative behavior is remedied. Self-reliance grows as more responsibility is delegated due to increased inner control and maturity demonstrated by the child.

Development of Maturity

A child's maturity level is a determining factor in his ability to learn. A child cannot be solely related to by the chronological age, but rather as a combination of varying age levels depending on the level of development in the following areas:

Motivation - reason to learn

Endeavor - effort or trying

Accomplishment - satisfaction of completion

The maturation process of the physical body does not necessarily coincide with the mental development or emotional control. Maturity level is directly proportionate to one's acceptance of responsibility. Self-discipline is a primary part in accomplishing this. The goal in developing maturity is to get a person to accept responsibility for one's own actions and change these without external pressure or monitoring. As the person experiences a small level of success and positive feedback, he/she is encouraged to apply more effort. If attempts have been thwarted or action is incomplete, a fear of failure causes a refusal to try again.

The natural tendency is to externalize and blame failure on others or circumstances. Forward motion is stopped by this rationalization: "If I don't try, I won't have to face that I can't do this." Perhaps all that is needed is another way of doing it, or a different attitude, or simply one more attempt. There are three major integrated aspects of mental maturation. These are self-image, self-reliance and self-discipline. A child can become discouraged when early attempts are criticized or are done for him/her. One learns in increments of small steps, by trial and error and through repetition. Allow improvement in attitude to follow a change in cooperative action. The child may hold resentment even when he/she has started moving in the right direction of appropriate conduct. Encourage the child to develop the reasoning capacity to problem solve and make decisions by giving opportunities to practice this. Build confidence by respecting his/her opinions. If the child is not given trust and allowed this in a non-judgmental space, interest will in time cease, as will his/her effort.

Chores and Responsibility

Responsibility is learned by competent completion of assigned tasks. Chores are important to train maturity and self-esteem. Make a list of expected duties of a certain chore. For example: help with meal, run sweeper, clean the bathroom, dust, rake leaves, clean up the yard or the garage. Work with the child at the start of training to show what a thorough job entails and what you expect to get the designated wage. This sets up a mini adult wok environment in which the child must do honest though work to get pay and maintain employment. Later in life, a boss will not nag your child to get work done. He/she will simply get fired and replaced by someone who will work effectively.

Cleaning his/her own room is expected each morning before school if the child wants to play out that afternoon. There is no chore money to keep his/her own immediate area and things clean and cared for. If this is not done, they will be put in the **Saturday Box**. If the room is not cleaned before school, all TV and play is on hold till it is finished. Work well done teaches pride of accomplishment and follow-through to completion. Money earned can teach monitory values and budget management to save for things the child especially desires.

Trial and error are swift teachers. Don't accept the child is inept. The project will have to be practiced until the child learns how to do a good job in a reasonable time. Do not accept less. It is easier at first to just do the work for the child or give up to their pursuit that they cannot do the project. Be reasonable. Trying for perfectionism discourages efforts ant trains neurosis. Remove privileges until work is finished. The child realizes that fun gets missed if I try to avoid work. It's hard at first, but worth it to teach good work habits.

Set up a **Chore Chart** with a certain chore each day Monday through Friday for each child in the family. These are to be done at a designated time such as before school or after school or before television. Have a set penalty if they are not done properly on time. No money is earned for chores you had to push to get done.

Motivation

Parents will find it more effective to motivate by incentive and reward, rather that punishment and intimidation. These harsh means are not effective long term. These work only until the person can get out from under your control or leave home. Everyone responds best to encouragement. People tend to live up to your expectations. Help by putting your focus on the right place. Concentrate on solutions, rather than problems. Where you put your energy is where the most gets done. Guide their efforts to finish a plan of action. Set up a specific chore or project chart with a start date and time of completion designated. Offer a reward or privilege based on success. Encourage perseverance to take them to pride of accomplishment. Many times, this is more rewarding than any prize or monetary gain. Teach consequences of action and be consistent.

The Benefits of Reward

Set up a specific reward and consequences so there are boundaries. If the child chooses not to do a chore, he/she is also choosing not to watch a favorite show or get reward credit for the chore. If the child complains or does a poor job or procrastinates do not give the agreed upon benefit or payment. This shows a direct consequence of action. Teach the choice of right action by your consistency of adherence to the rule. If you set a plan and don't follow it, you are training your child to do this in other areas of their life.

Prepare your child for later challenges by demonstrating the 'Law of Correct Choice.' – Right choice = desired results; Poor choices = undesirable results. Appropriate choices increase the options of freedom. If a child is shielded from the consequence of their actions, they learn controlling behaviors that complicate their personal relations later.

Play and Learning Activities for Families

* Sharing time together is the best reward for stars earned from shores or improved behavior or incorporated virtues. Here is a list of ideas:
* Learn to play the guitar or other musical instrument.
* Go ice skating or roller skating.
* Paint together on paper or a mural or color in a coloring book.
* Attend a sporting event.
* Go to events at your local community center.
* Learn to cook together.
* Learn to dance and go together.
* Plan a slumber party.
* Go swimming.
* Go fishing or lay a ball game together.
* Plant a garden or a flower or some herbs.
* Declutter your clothes and personal things and find a family to donate the to.
* Go to a museum.
* Take a nature hike. Make a collage of leaves and seeds you collect.
* Exercises together.
* Play cards, scrabble or another game.
* Read a story. Make up a story and write it down. Visit a bookstore
* Ask older family members to tell stories of their youth.
* Watch the stars and moon at night.
* Get out your family albums. Research your history.
* Make crafts as gifts and tree ornaments.
* Have party to celebrate a TV week free.
* Attend community concerts and events or organize a community clean-up.

Teaching by Example: Do the things you want your children to do.

* Know yourself (your strengths, challenges, dreams, motivations).
* Follow your heart.
* Be true to yourself.
* Treat all beings (including yourself) with respect.
* Use moderation in all things.
* Live within your means saving a percent of your income.
* Direct negative emotions out by going for a walk.
* Use praise to motivate and build self-love.
* Make decisions in advance rather than spur of the moment.
* Balance time for play and work.
* Finish what you start.
* Establish firm boundaries that others are not allowed to cross.
* Set goals and follow them.
* Share mealtime with loved ones in happy conversations.
* Take three deep breaths before you discuss important topics.
* Talk and listen to your loved ones.
* Say what you want instead of what you don't want.
* Acknowledge efforts to do a better job and improve.

Someone will establish your children's values.

Will it be you?

Is your home a place of harmony were basic values of respect are practiced? Even though your children may grow up and establish a life with different values than yours, give them a basis for comparison with a foundation of integrity. Without this, our youth float at the mercy of circumstance. Then the pressure of the peer culture will set their codes of behavior, standards and values. Be kind, firm and consistent to establish self-discipline. No one has ever decided in anger or resentment to become a more considerate, productive individual.

Setting Rules and Boundaries

Train the importance of boundaries. If the adults raising the child don't require respect of their boundaries, the child won't respect others right of boundaries. Let the child know that property is to be respected also. The child loses something he/she values if others property is broken aimlessly or on purpose. By being inconsistent, adults cause anxiety because the children do not know what to expect or where the boundaries are. If you tell the child" I need quiet time or space", claim your right of boundary to be left alone for a while.

Use the following guidelines to objectively set reasonable rules:

Set a time limit for the rule to be followed. For example:

Do this chore before you go to school or right after supper. You only have five minutes left to be in bed with your teeth brushed.

Time limits help clarify if the rule has been followed and reduces disputes and confusion. Consistency is more important than severity.

There needs to be consequences every time the rule is broken. This is to be explained ahead as a regular, indisputable course of action to be followed through without lengthy dissertations. The less talk, the better. Consequences are meant to be reasonable. Punishment can be too severe. It could create guilt in the adult and won't be carried out. If it is followed through, then other concessions are made later from guilt which further impede consistency.

Discuss in *Family Council* why certain rules are important? Ask the children how they think the rules will help them now and later in life. Ask each child to repeat the rule and explain it so he/she can't argue it was not heard later. This is a effective control mechanism of children. To say "I didn't know what you meant "or "I didn't hear."

The next step is to let the child remember to follow the rule on his/her own. If the adult reminds the child, the responsibility has shifted, and the child is not being allowed to think for himself or herself. The child learns security as it is understood the adult means what is said. Be kind, firm and consistent to establish self-discipline.

Action/Reaction

Attempting to consistently apply a bad rule will result in resentment and angry attacks by both the child and the adult. Inconsistent application of a good rule will result in lack of control to accomplish desired training. Basically, you will be teaching the child to push limits in life and get by with whatever he/she can.

Write up a chart of the rules, time limits and consequences and post it in a place the child will easily see. Read it together. For instance:

Arguing after asking twice - *Write "I respect the rules." (5 times)*

Leaving a mess - *Practice picking it up for 5 min.*

Chore is not completed – *Miss the next play privilege.*

Rowdy in house or car - *5 min. in the Quiet Chair. Put this in an out-of-the-way spot.*

Unreasonable fighting during playing game - *Game is over.*

Yelling - *Repeat five times "I speak in pleasant voice tones."*

Whining - *Person will not get what he/she is whining for at that time.*

Persistent bad manners at meal - *Wait to eat until others are finished.*

If the child misbehaves in public, it is to be dealt with immediately, just as at home. Remove planned privileges. If children are fighting in the car, stop immediately and pull over. Tell them it is not safe to drive with their distractions. If they continue, simply turn around and go home, pulling over and stopping every time they start being rowdy again. The adults may lose a recreational event or even a vacation, but it won't happen many times if consistently followed though. It is better for the adult to be home relaxing peace fully than on an outing in turmoil with disrespectful, unruly children. If negative behavior persists, go home and put child to bed for one hour. Excursions are a luxury in life, not a requirement. These are earned by acceptable behavior.

The basis for effective rule setting is agreement between adults. Children are gamblers. They play the odds relative to how much they can get away with. Getting by with something 50% of the time is worth the try if the reward is worth the risk.

Creative Training (Compliments and Consistency)

The purpose of discipline is to allow freedom to all individuals rather than restrict freedom. Discipline is a process of learning inner control through self-awareness so that a person can have a happy, fruitful life. The main consideration is to communicate respect and to teach the child to do this also in all relationships in his /her lifetime.

* **Compliment children more often.** Concentrate on the good things the child does. The inappropriate behavior cannot be ignored; yet spend as little time as possible correcting it in a monotone firm voice giving the designated consequence. Be consistent so the child learns consistency and order.
* **Spend quality time with each child every day playing and talking. This is a priority.**
* Write a *Sprinklet Qualities List* of each family member and read daily. This builds confidence and a positive self-image. Be honest genuine and sincere.
* Write a note each day telling something special to your child and place under his/her pillow or in the lunch pail. Write I love you.
* Rest daily and pace yourself so you have patience and endurance.
* Maximize self-reliance, cooperation and responsibility. Work at the solution side of a situation, rather than the problem.
* Don't do anything to someone you wouldn't want done to you.
* Avoid phrases that denote external control. For example state:
* "I'm asking you to do your homework now." rather than ordering "Get busy!" Anger comes from lack of control and harsh, unfair, disrespectful treatment.
* Ask authoritatively, rather than order.
* Be firm and consistent.
* Realize we all make mistakes while practicing for excellence.
* Life is earning freedom and privilege by assuming responsibility.
* Give a *Peace Award* at each family council meeting to the person who made the greatest effort to be peaceful that week. Post the award on their door. (Use special paper for their certificate.)

Rewards and Contracts

To set up the **Star Chart**, list three behaviors the child needs to improve. He/she is to agree on these from family council discussion or they will be resented as external control and judgmental. The child will feel like he/she is under the spotlight to be fixed. To incorporate participation, present this as self-control the child can learn to make his/her life more successful. Each three-hour period that the child goes without the negative behavior, a star can be put on the star chart. Let the child help make this colorful with stickers and drawings. Also let the child put on the earned stars. Praise the progress. Just state in a matter of fact tone "No star for this three-hour time frame" when the child participates in the target behavior.

Avoid giving time and words to reprimands. If this inappropriate behavior is done in the first five minutes, the whole three hours remains before there is another chance. This will motivate the child to put more effort in the next time. These three-hour segments of time go from rising until 12 hours later so four stars can be earned each day.

The improvement in the child's environment is a noted benefit.

Set up a **Goody Box** with things under $2 that the child has gone shopping to purchase as rewards for the stars he earns on the **Star Chart**. (The child does not buy these with his/her own money.) This is not a prize or gift because the child earns the reward. When 20 stars are earned, the child may draw a reward out of The **Goody Box** of his choice. Keep about three to five choices in the box to make it an ongoing motivation.

A **Behavioral Contract** is an effective means to improve behavior. Two people participate in the agreement written as such:

Terms of Agreement: Rewards are agreed upon as follows:

If I fulfill my part of the contract, I will receive the herein written agreed upon rewards. I agree that if I do not fulfill my part of the contract, the rewards will be withheld. Signed_____

Each person has a contract set up this way (Make two copies.)

Respect and Organization

All items left lying around after evening pickup go in a **Saturday Box.** (This Saturday Box is a box from which things can only be reclaimed on Sat. and cost 25 cents each. Stop buying new toys until the child takes care & respects the one's he/she has. Train cleanliness. Traits of organization & time management begin with order.

Listen to what the child is saying. There may be a just complaint.

Set up a **'time out chair'** in an out of the way area. This is to be out of range of toys cell phone, video games and TV. The chair is required when there are unkind actions. Set a timer for five minutes for the child to consider being respectful and kind.

Even a very young child learns to sit in the chair until the bell rings. This will take supervision at first to firmly place the child back in the chair when he/she gets out before the bell rings. Be certain to take the child out as soon as the bell rings so he equates this as the time to be through with the restriction. After the discipline is established to keep the child in the chair, do not start the time until the child is sitting quietly.

This penalty is only used for relationship interaction that is not respectful of others space and feelings. The concept is when you act unkind, you get removed from others to think about being more respectful to them. This can be used for yelling, hitting, playing too rough or unfair, talking back and breaking or bothering other's things.

Allow the child to cry or be unhappy. Restrict the place for this to be in his own room so there will be privacy if the child really needs to express emotions to integrate the experience. The child is not to be sent to his/her room as a punishment. This teaches it is not ok to express your feelings and you will be punished for having them. He/she can come out of their room at will as soon as they are calmed down. This stops the use of crying to control others, manipulate and be a general nuisance carrying on and on

Set up a place for whining. This could be located on a certain chair out the way of the general flow of the family. Say to the child, "Use your words so I can understand what you want." If the child keeps following you around whining, say to him or her, "I guess you want to go to the whining place. You can stay there as long as you want and then come and tell me what you want when you are ready." Whining in my family meant that you were not getting what you were requesting until it was done in a respectful tone of voice.

Important Factors in Goal Setting

* Rise above the discouraging opinions of others.
* The best way to counter criticism and putdowns is to succeed.
* Rather than thinking you had a bad day accept, "I had a 'character building' day today."
* Surround yourself with people who believe in you.
* Have patient and consistent forward motion. Respond to life with more ease.
* Find ways to serve people. Do something for someone and don't tell anyone.
* Be personally responsible for your dream. No one will ever care more about your dream than you do.
* Replace old habits of reaction with new habits of perspective.
* Live softer, more gracefully and life is more compatible.
* Make peace with imperfection. Desire tranquility.
* Focus on solutions, rather than on problems.
* Focus on the pastime of gratitude.
* Notice what is happening in your head before your thoughts build momentum.

Goal Setting for the Family

Family togetherness comes through a cooperative effort of all the members striving toward specific goals which fulfill everyone's needs. Setting weekly goals to willingly strive to give one another more freedom and consideration will incorporate mutual respect.

The point of value to remember is that family members need to accept equal responsibility for peaceful coexistence. Too many individuals with differing goals will end in turmoil and trauma.

For this plan to work, adults must allow freedom for each person to think and take action for himself/herself. Smother love dictates that you must live *my* goals for your life to make me happy to have peace between us. Guilt and personal goal setting don't go together. To avoid this, set up a convenient time which fits into all the family member's schedules for a *Family Council Meeting* each week. Have a box with a slit in the top called The *Suggestion Box* can hold ideas for improvement contributed "by everyone for the good of everyone."

Each person writes three suggestions for improvement.

List three main obstacles and three solutions to overcome these.

Each person writes three long term plans for one year from now.

Discuss these at Family Council Meeting and devise plans to support one another to implement these positive actions. Make a list of the guidelines for the group and post for all to conveniently see. These are not to be directed at any certain person or resentment results.

Create a mental picture of yourself with the desired result already accomplished.

Use affirmation statements that your goals have been reached & repeat each twenty-one times daily. New habit patterns are formed in repetitions of 21. Example of this are:

I have excellent comprehension.

I speak only kind supportive words.

Treasure Mapping is an effective and fun way to visualize your goals. Cut pictures out of old magazines of the things you want. Make a scrap book and imagine you have already attained these in your life.

Positive Poster Thoughts

Write any of these on small signs and place in visible spots around the house:

I listen carefully

I treat others like I want to be treated

I practice success daily

Joy fills my heart

I am free and give others their freedom

I see the good in me and you

Stand on your own feet, not on someone else

We are a family of love

Smile

Every day I learn more about being kinder

Prepare to prevent

Have a good day

Compliments help

Humor heals so lighten up

Ask rather than order

Giving comes back in special blessings

Love directs my path

Forgiveness works miracles

Suggested Activities at Close of the Day

* Read a list of the good qualities of each family member.
* Concentrate on a list of what you have to be thankful for.
* Read a Story together.
* Envision your goals fulfilled.
* Look at your treasure maps together.
* See love and light surrounding your life.
* Give hugs as you tuck your children in bed.

The Price

When parents want to make life easy and free of problems for their child, it doesn't prepare them to handle difficulties in life. When sheltered too much, they don't learn the fundamental principles of taking care of one's self. Life is harder because coping skills are not taught to wait for things and to appreciate them. The child lives in a fairy tale world of overprotection and doesn't grow up emotionally. When large difficulties come, they can seem impossible to solve, because they haven't had any experiences handling conflicts.

A child needs to be allowed to express his/her opinion. A child needs to be allowed to try and fail and try again. This teaches how to make decisions. Even though the adults may do it faster and better, the self-image of the child will be diminished if everything is done for them. They are unprepared to face adult challenges and persevere.

The price the child pays for overindulgence and spoiling is too great.

Dear Mom and Dad (Written by an anonymous child)

I wouldn't trade you for Tommy's dad for all the money in the world. Tommy's dad brings homework from the office every night and even on weekends. They never go anywhere together, not to the zoo, or fishing, or to play ball in park. I like the way you talk to me when I am down or upset. You always make me see that things aren't so bad and that they will get better, (Which they always do eventually.) I like the way you don't let me get away with much. Sometimes I act mad when I don't get my way, but deep down I am glad you are teaching me discipline. I would be scared to death if you let me do anything I want with no limits.

I like it that you and Mom agree on the rules. If Tommy asks one of his parents and they say "No", he just goes and asks the other one. He always gets his way. I don't think life will always be like that and he won't know how to handle it. I'm glad you and Mom don't fight. Kids get upset when their mom and dad can't get along together. I like the way you tell me the truth about everything. When I grow up and have kids, I want to be just like you.

I love you,

Jimmy

The Prophet

by Khaliah Gibran

Your Children are not your children

They are the sons and daughters of Life's longing for itself.

They come through you, but not from you.

And though they are with you, yet they belong not to you.

You may give them your love, but not your thoughts.

For they have their own thoughts.

You may house their bodies, but not their souls.

For their souls dwell in the house of tomorrow.

Which you cannot visit, not even in your dreams.

You may strive to be like them,

but seek not to make them be like you.

For life goes not backward nor tarries with yesterday.

You are the bows from which your children,

as living arrows, are sent forth.

Let your bending of the archer's bow be in gladness.

SECTION THREE

Teens in These Troubled Times

Chapter Eleven: The Teen's Search for Self

Teens are under more stress from cultural conditions and identity challenges than earlier generations. In their search for life direction in these troubled times, they need to learn how to establish a new life plan with boundaries, positive thoughts, feelings and actions to manifest the greatest good. Reduction in stress can affect improvement in brain function, health, emotional balance and energy levels. Integration of mind, body and spirit comes through merging into the highest expression of one's potential.

The 'Ultimate Self' is recovered in a reunion with unconditional self-love. The personal journey of the teens search for self-reveals beliefs and false realities which challenge core values. Purifying the consciousness of fear, anger and guilt patterns facilitates a re-orientation of the memory base and self- concept. Self-awareness, goal setting, mindfulness, focusing imageries, NLP, Self-hypnosis, vibrational and art therapy are introduced as tools to enhance internal control with coping skills and self-directives.

The following techniques are presented:

- Processes to build motivation, organization skills, follow through and self-sustainability.
- Self- questioning to create balance in life for health, clarity, joy, peace and productivity.
- Guidance to find freedom to be authentic and self-confident
- Survival skills based in safety, independent action and personal need fulfillment.
- Imagery to provide self-acknowledgment and inner knowing.
- Breathing exercises to access a constant source within of comfort and protection
- The benefits of these aid maturity in these areas:
- Clear the memory base and incorporate a more successful life using self-hypnosis
- Assist self-discovery and improves relationships.
- Balance the left/right brain to rejuvenate creativity and potential.
- Claim self-empowerment and start living life from inner direction
- Learn self-dialoging skills using affirmations and imagery

Considerations that influence At Risk Behaviors in Teens and Pre-teens:

(Note these are not causes of At-Risk Behavior, but in case studies have been patterns).

Poor parenting	History of behavioral problems
Higher social economic standard	Structure and communication in the home
Attitudes and beliefs of parents	Teen pregnancy
Students failure patterns academically	Single parent homes
Teens who are not on a college track	Peer pressure (Alcohol, drugs, violence, bullying)

Theory of Teen Development: Family and Social Influences

Teen depression, crime and suicide abound in communities all over the USA. Half of America's adolescents are at some risk for serious problems from their accident-prone lifestyles. There are new risks that their parents and grandparents didn't have to face. The increase in substance use and sexual activity is due to breakdown in family communication, peer pressure, changes in cultural and social norms and rebellion.

The book entitled "A Tribe Apart" follows the lives of several teenager's daily lives and thoughts. The author, Patricia Hersch reports that about a quarter of all adolescents have engaged in behaviors that are harmful or dangerous to themselves or others. These behaviors include getting pregnant, using drugs, taking a part in antisocial activity and failing at school. These behaviors are also being tracked in younger and younger children.

Schools are tense, rigid and militant. Metal detectors and police are placed in schools.

Seventh graders are faced with intimidation by their upper classmates. Bully behavior is common in groups that form clicks, threatening physical abuse to anyone who crosses them. Students are stuffing other kids in lockers and trash cans. Stealing, carrying weapons, fighting, verbal and physical abuse are normal nowadays. Self-image is declining Teachers are underpaid and lack the training to deal with the explosion of corrupt behaviors on the school grounds. Pestlet behaviors are on the rise.

Drugs are so readily available; drug peddlers are their friends and have a variety of substance choices right in class. Tough guys and street gangs are the role models in many schools. The gangs are becoming an alternative to family due to a decline of family unity and interaction. The struggle to find their place in all this unrest is escalating.

The most stunning change for adolescents today is their aloneness. The teen culture has isolated themselves in media contact with the internet and video games that walls them off from social interaction. This lack of intimacy in their relationships creates an inability to experience joy from physical contact. Relationship bonding from safe touching that comes from a healthy sense of self-love is seldom mutually enjoyed. Students at school are becoming dehumanized living in collective isolation.

Children are raised in these busy times in a careless negligent manner. Rushing creates extreme anxiety. Many of our children are not rebelling or avoiding the parents; in many cases, the adults simply aren't there. Teens are spending the majority of their time with others who are not their parents. Statistics continue to show the shocking breakdown in the family unit. In one class of the interviewed students, the teacher did a survey of the twenty-eight students, and found that 75% of them had breakfast alone or with siblings they were responsible for.

One fourth of the seventh graders in the group made dinner for the family. Dale Blyth, of the Search Institute, relates the effect goes beyond issues of rules and discipline to the idea exchanges between generations that do not occur; conversations are not held; the guidance and role modeling is not taking place. This may be due to single working parents or a home in which both parents are working to meet financial concerns. Loving Sprinklet is a way for generations to keep the lines of communication open.

Sarah Larson, social historian, said that no matter what economic class, homes used to be full of people most of the day when several generations lived together. Longer life independence and senior living centers are replacing multi-generational family homes. With the requirement of two working parents and daily stress, adults don't take the time to lead their children as thoroughly through the process of growing up.

A report by Carnegie Council on Adolescent Development reports that many teens spend virtually all of their discretionary time without companionship or supervision by responsible adults. One of the most relevant factors in the lack of family interaction is poor communication and the decrease in common interests. The distance between the family generations is broadening and they find less and less to talk about. The goal in all communication is mutual respect. Building self-esteem is the biggest factor in satisfactory communication. Prioritizing their daily activities can cut down on overload to address this crisis mode living and improve communication. Prioritizing their daily activities can cut down on overload to address this crisis mode living and improve communication. Emphasis is on the necessity of making another person feel important by listening to them. Communication is a learned process in which we use the elements of our bodies, sense organs, brains, expectations, and values. Developing intimacy connects people to the ability to have clear honest communication. Keeping communication lines open can prevent rifts and buried emotions which end in passive aggressive behaviors. Honesty Sprinklet is willing to look at the truth of every situation.

Listening well is the key to what you hear. The voice may be loud, soft, high, low, clear, muffled, slow or fast. Most people don't hear how they really sound, but only how they intend to sound. When the communication has declined to hateful jabs, family members or peers involved in these interactions begin to resent each other and find faults. Picking at each other and criticism begins to undermine the trust at the core of the friendship. This is another reason each person pulls away and spends less time with one another. They are unaware of their motives and actions. Many people are unaware of their unconscious thoughts, motives and subliminal communication. Many things are not put into words that are communicated in body language and attitudes. Kindness Sprinklet comments on the mice things others do.

Virginia Satir, author of "Communication: Talking and Listening," expresses, "Communication is the largest single factor determining what kinds of relationships a person makes with others and what happens to us in the world." Satir relates the level of self-worth as the "pot level." This is the range of communication of giving and receiving and is learned to a large extent by the age of five years old. Early learning becomes the foundation for the rest of our lives unless something powerful intercedes. Accident trauma, divorce and war can alter the influence of the first five years in negative ways. The self-responsible reprogramming tools such as these offered in this booklet can intervene in a positive manner to create better outcomes.

Violence is on the rise in youth, in the media and the world at large. A report by the Department of Education said, "Violent and unruly behavior peaked in eight and ninth grades and the approximately 70% of weapons found in public school are found in middle schools. Bonding even comes in the form of violence. Teens feel music is a way to connect, whether it is rock, heavy metal, or rap. It overrides the painful self-consciousness of adolescence by easing the need for suave interactions and creating an instant community among listeners. Youth are seeking community and the larger community of adults must reach out with alternatives.

University of Michigan's "Monitoring the Future Study" reports that by 8th grade, 67% of youth report having tried alcohol, 13% marijuana and 56% smoke cigarettes. The pressures teens are under now from violent media desensitizing, sex-oriented commercials, unfit role models and constant safety risks seem insurmountable. The common acceptance these days that virginity lasts only until a young girl is thirteen. It is understandable with parties with alcohol and drugs and no supervision.

This goes back to the lack of intimacy in childhood and social pressure to conform to casual relationships. In the breakdown of communication, parents either won't let their teens talk about their opinions or turn a blind eye to the severity of their kid's actions due to denial or overload. Many parents are too overwhelmed with their own lives, jobs and bad marriages to notice the lack of involvement in their kid's lives. Families don't do things together, nor even eat at the same table. Adolescents who are having trouble are in need of love, respect and attention. There is a growing need to train the concepts of Sprinklets and Pestlets.

One of the biggest problems to emerge in teenage society is acceptance. Many get rejected or reject others because of style, looks, political beliefs and religious beliefs. Many of today's youth need guidance to achieved identification in the midst of so many dangerous choices. Teens should all start looking at the inner self and take time to look at the real person underneath. Bulling has become rampant in schools as a way to deal with ones' inner pestlets.

Troubled kids are giving a cry for help to their families who should be stricter. The kids feel the parents don't care, so why should they care? Hersch reports, "It seems the family is not the only powerful predictor of adolescent choices. A good kid, with family support, will do bad things less often. "In *Healthy Communities Healthy Youth*, the Search Institute discovered care and support within the family spill over the family's borders. If the community does not assume responsibility for all its children through strong supportive programs for all kids, the teen statistics of crime drugs and pregnancy will increase.

The saddest part of the teen culture is their loss of hope. They fend for themselves, when their world would have felt safer, more certain if they had some clear rules to follow. Today's teens form their own community support. They help each other through the bad times such as divorces, abuse, date rape and violence, drug overdose and all sorts of things that affect them. By the time they are seniors, their innocence is long-gone, and many feel their destiny is about to be sealed. More programs are needed which offer a format of guidance programs that include personal, peer, family and community support. Truly the core of restoring family unity is to reconnect with the elders who hold the knowledge of our roots and heritage. In this way youth will connect with their roots and heritage and have a clearer understanding of where they chose for the future to take them.

Values in the family reflect a priority of the necessity to live these principals. If we want kindness, we must use kind words. If we want to stop violence in our youth, we have to stop being violent in the home and give them a peaceful place to return. Even if there is a strong foundation, there are temptations in the changing cultural environment. If we want to impact less delinquency and gang pressure, we need to provide a vision of the family as a loving unit with parents who show themselves and the teens more respect. This will offer teens an avenue to build self-esteem and authenticity within themselves. Some of the following behaviors are descriptive of normal teens, but watch for extremes:

Teens feelings are easily hurt due to hormonal changes and modern-day stress. They have a desire to be more independent from family and at the same time need to be nurtured and protected. Normally they do have a need for privacy and time alone to sort out all the rapid changes in themselves and the culture. Note if this is obsessive or if they tend to demand privileges and avoid responsibilities.

Teens have a high level of emotional and physical energy combined with long periods of 'hanging out' and doing nothing productive by adult standards. A delicate balance must be struck between honoring the importance of their own self-discovery and their friends and asserting adult responsibilities. Avoid confusing contradictive statements such as these: When they try to pursue adult activities, we tell them "You are too young." When they act their age, we tell them to "Stop behaving like children."

Although teens may be reluctant to get too involved with grownups, encourage discussing their experiences with family members and teachers. Teens are trying to find their own values apart from those held by their families and they are testing boundaries. Make sure there is someone to objectively listen to them so that they are not turning to violent and immoral role models. Keep the lines of communication open.

The changes during adolescence and the teen years are filled with parental expectation, sexual discovery, experimentations and the identity crisis of personality development. The process of maturity is complicated amidst peer pressure and a collapsing cultural environment. In most cases this is the transition from the safety of being the protected child whose security is provided to being cast into facing the outside world alone. In other situations of lack of parent and adult supervision, the teen this cast into the harsh struggle of survival at even younger ages.

Emotionalism and mood swings mark the psychological, hormonal and rapid growth. There is a tendency to look at ones' own faults and weakness while dwelling on the exceptional qualities and strengths of others. When a healthy self-concept is established, the teen accepts

that each person has special abilities but needs help in clarifying goals to develop this. Life lessons come through the process of making mistakes and learning from them. Experience has always been the best teacher. Respect is the main factor in accepting authority. Each generation has this same process at different levels. Guidance comes from many sources.

True friends are a buffer to all these pressures and changes. Needs change quickly, but one factor remains consistent. This is the importance of true friends who share interests, have our back, lets us be ourselves and grow into our strengths a d potential... A true friend is honest and can be counted upon no matter what A teen must be his/her own best friend. Being in a relationship of mutual respect with parents also provides a higher chance of successfully surviving trying times. It is important that each individual decide who he/she is rather than accepting the beliefs of others. Looking within keeps one from coming the captive prisoner of a false self-concept projected from the environment. The teen then losses control of his/her life choices. Hurtful things others have said become hot buttons. These erroneous beliefs take away personal freedom.

Stereotyping is a form of external control. If certain prejudices are taught from early childhood, free thought is hampered. It is important to analyze these beliefs of races, roles, classes, and expectation of the roles of men and women. Make a list of these and revaluate any concepts which do not bring your life in balance with truth. These are things that one has accepted as truth and repeats in self-talk in their own thoughts and self-image.

Author, Susan Korones Gifford, takes a position that the self-talk many individuals use reminds them that they don't measure up. She quotes authority sources of educators and authors who all substantiate that this inner critic can pick away at the person's ego until it is all but diminished with negative, self-assessments. Gifford gives logical support by the example of the inner critic who may have been buzzing in your ear so persistently with derogatory comments about your hair and weight, that she's a part of the background noise of your life. She relates if you're a perfectionist, this inner critic will nitpick your every effort. This pattern must stop to avoid upsetting social situations and work performance. The author's information accurately relates instances in a logical manner which express the damage of being a fault-finding perfectionist. Dwelling on one's pestlet qualities leads to depression and anxiety.

Gifford states that this inner voice can be helpful, but it takes constructive self-appraisal to be an asset and allay. A person with low self-esteem and self-blaming conduct is vulnerable to the opinions of others. In this vulnerable state, messages from unreliable sources can be absorbed which are not valid. All internal dialogue needs discernment. Knowing where negative thoughts originate can help you understand why you are having them. The appraisal of others may become so internalized that a person can lose his/her own opinions. The following imageries give specific tools for replacing behavioral habits of focusing on what is wrong by challenging and contradicting your inner critic and turning the self-talk into a rational, realistic voice of encouragement.

Teenagers have the challenge of being internally or externally directed in today's world of turmoil. Each person has a choice to let peer pressure get to him or establish a sense of self within. This ten-step process is structured to build self-esteem, establish quality of life. A variety of topics are experienced to encourage self-confidence to create a life of independence in which the teen can more successfully function in the "Present Moment" with greater joy and connection to realize true self-worth and purpose.

What each person is ultimately seeking is found in the center of one's own being. Psychological balance of peace depends on how deeply and firmly one is established in this center. Primitive cultures had survival as their major priority, so they were naturally connected to the elements and the source of nature's supply. In modern times, we have exchanged our priority from survival, frugality and feeling to success, acquisition and conformity.

Chapter Twelve: Troubled Teen Characteristics and At-Risk Behaviors

No matter what happens with these young adolescents, something is always wrong. They are moody, forgetful, irresponsible, impolite, loud, overly self–absorbed and generally have anti-social behavior. Those who are more at-risk are skipping classes, have a low sense of self-worth, are alienated from the mainstream and have excessive anger and anxiety.

Interpersonal interaction needs to target the theses areas of development: Information to help teens with life's pressure including training in assertiveness, communication with peers and adults, stress reduction, social coping skills and general confidence building. Teens normally consider themselves members of distinct groups such as jocks, preppies, gangs. Note these groups have specific values, attitudes and leisure time activities.

Plan a strategy to stay involved with your teen and build family traditions. Inventory relevant resources in your area. Parents are faced with so many outside influences that can affect their teens that it is important to avoid overload. Plan less activity and organize your time for a balance of work, play, rest and sleep. Be tolerant of yourself and everyone else in hard times. Deal with stress from your center within just as you are training your teens to do.

More Advice for Parents of Teens: Being Me Letting You Be You

It is especially hard to release those you love from your expectation of what you feel is right and what is best for them. This is based on the parent's limited perspective of their own experience and goals for the children. This does not allow for their dreams and growth process through trial, error and struggles. The parent or educator can relate from unrealized dreams of their own or cultural and ancestral programming, List any limiting beliefs you may still have.

— Being My Own Friend as Well as a Parent: What am I role modeling?
— Am I taking care of myself?
— Am I being my authentic self?
— Am I being a martyr?
— Am I being a victim?
— Am I being sick for attention?
— Am I being happy?

— Am I being a leader?

— Am I taking a firm stand?

— Am I setting boundaries?

— Am I honoring myself?

— Am I passing on the family stories?

— Am I carrying on family traditions?

— Am I establishing new family traditions?

— Am I conducting family rituals?

Imagery for Teens and Their Families

We tend to be one place and have our thoughts somewhere else.as we think about something other than what we are doing. We are not in our center which distracts focus causes us to and miss the full experience. It is critical to be fully present in what is happening at that time. The past and the future distort the appreciation of this experience.

The next imagery is designed to help a person become more engaged in the moment and to be able to live from your Loving Sprinklet center.

Take three deep breaths inhaling through the nose and exhaling through the mouth. Begin to rock as if you are rocking a little child with your eyes closed. Experience a warmth in your heart from a violet light in the center of your chest. This emits comfort and peace to convert all fears and pain that have been stored in your heart. Just be in the stillness with this little child in the violet energy. This is your comforting heart flame and you are nurturing your own 'Inner Child.' Be there for this little one. Count to five and return to alert awareness bringing with you a sense of being centered in inner nurturing. 1-2-3-4-5. Move your fingers and toes as you return to Beta awareness.

Finding Calm in Chaos with Teens

When there is turmoil surrounding you, close your eyes and visualize you are in the eye of a hurricane where all is still and quiet. Get in nature and let everything go that is not peaceful.

Finding Answers When You Are Under Pressure Taking an Exam

Close your eyes and use your breath to go into your head brain. You have all the answers in a book inside your head containing important facts. Access this. Count to five and open your eyes. Feel relaxed with answers available as you write your first response to questions:

Imagery: Inner Sanctuary of Personal Safety

Begin by getting in a comfortable position and closing your eyes. Focus on your breath by inhaling to the count of five through our nose and exhaling through the mouth to the count of five. Begin to visualize a luminous white light coming through the top of your head. This clearing energy has frequency of every color to clear all your cells. It washes all negativity from you mind and all stress from your muscles. Relax your facial muscles, your shoulders and chest, arms, trunk, legs and feet. Press your fingertips together and curl your toes. Hold and release three times to aid this full body relaxation. Next rotate your feet and extend them. Curl them up and release. Let go of all tension physically, mentally and emotionally.

A protective shield is created by the white light which now floods in all directions around you. It makes you feel alert and energetic as all heaviness leaves your body. You are in control of your emotions and mental abilities. Your body systems are operating at optimal capacity. Safety enfold you in this sanctuary within.

Inhale to the count of seven and exhale to the count of nine. This moves stale air out of the lungs and activates and revitalizes your whole system and brain function. Come back to alert awareness on the count of five bringing back this sense of safety

1-2-3-4-5. Move your fingers and toes as you return to Beta awareness.

Chapter Thirteen: Being Me Letting You Be You

Being Your Better Self: The Together Self

Unveil new levels of joy and bliss by balancing work, rest and play. Enhance your senses of seeing, feeling, hearing, speaking and intuition. In this next process you will be using a combination of art therapy and self-hypnosis to construct a shield of your Together Self. This shield is who you are in your heart sanctuary centered in unconditional self-love and respect.

Get comfortable and close your eyes to go into this center within. Use your breath as a bridge of entry. Focus on a golden light in the center of your forehead that is getting larger and larger with each breath. With every breathe you go deeper and deeper within this space. Now go back in your thoughts to see yourself as a small child. Only positive images come to you in this experience of self-recovery. In your self-talk give this child words of encouragement and praise for all the effort that has been involved in growing up. Continue this imagery for about two minutes and then focus on the best qualities that are in this child of curiosity and adventure. Bond with yourself as the inner child and the yourself at your current age. Come back to alert awareness on the count of five bringing back the vitality and innocence of this child that you hold in your heart center. 1-2-3-4-5.

Now make a Power Shield of this 'Together Self' using bright colors of colored pencils and tempera paint. Draw symbols and pictures that represent your successes and good qualities. Keep this shield in a special place to remind you of this place of safety and personal inner power.

Set up a journal and make notes on your imageries. In this journal, draw a picture of a staircase. On each stair write something you have overcome in life. All change comes in small steps. Every 21 days add at least one thing you have mastered in this staircase of your growth.

Art Activities for Re-Scripting and Self-Awareness

Activity One: This is a combination of Psycho-cybernetics, NLP, Hypno-therapy, Art Therapy and Color Therapy. Get comfortable and close your eyes. Go into light alpha using the breath cycle of inhaling to the count of four and exhaling to the count of four. Repeat four times. Count backwards from ten to one as you imagine you are going deeper within to your heart center. Visualize a loving experience in a family unit. Continue this imagery about three minutes. Come back with memories of an early life growing up with Sprinklets. 1-2-3-4-5. Draw a picture of this experience with the sprinklets involved.

Activity Two: Journal your images and emotions as you recall these.

   Journal your feelings and awareness of this time.

   You in your toddler years

   You in your elementary years

   You in your teen years

Activity Three: Rather than dwell on pestlet times, recreate a sprinklet experience if you didn't see any. Draw a positive picture of you in each period of maturation up to your current age. Let your intuitive mind choose the colors to express. You can rewrite the script of any pestlet memories and emotions for each time frame by drawing pictures of yourself in situations filled with memories of joy, love, security, peace and other sprinklets.

   Now you are ready to emotionally restructure each of the five images by looking at the pleasant scenarios of each time frame. Reconstruct and experience positive emotions associated with these rewritten memories.

Understanding the Adolescent Brain

   Dr. Jay Giedd, chief of brain imaging at National Institute of Mental Health has studied over 1,800 teens and reports that the brain doesn't fully mature for ration decision making before the late teens or early 20's. The results show that the prefrontal cortex is the last to mature, typically between ages 18 to 21 years old. This explains why teenagers find it difficult to reason, plan and make decisions.

The Effects of Drugs and Alcohol on the Brain

   The use of drugs to calm or mask emotions is ever growing in the teen population. David Friedman, PhD of Washington University School of Medicine in St. Louis, MO reports drugs change the way the brain works. When drugs interfere with the delicate mechanisms through which nerve cells transmit, receive and process biochemically, the person loses the ability to control their own lives. Cocaine is opiate that turns on the pleasure circuit allowing the pleasure endorphin dopamine to accumulate in the nerve synapse. These same centers control memory and emotions. Addictive use causes a reduction in the number of neuron receptor cells causing down regulation. This may explain the craving and withdrawal symptoms of extreme depression, violent behavior, hallucinations and paranoia. Seizures, heart attacks and strokes have also resulted from continued use.

Heroin is another opiate that binds immediately with the receptors of the neurons in the brain causing a euphoric state of relaxation. Side effects include nausea, vomiting, drowsiness, mood swings and infections from contaminated needle. The biggest danger is that these same opiate receptors control breathing causing it to slow down or stop working altogether. Thousands of people have died after their breathing stops from a heroin overdose. The hallucinogenic PCP blocks the way some receptors communicate to the inside of the cell. A major concern about this dug is the unpredictability of it effects. It can cause aggression, passivity disorganized thinking and hostility from one dose to the next.

Cocaine is a stimulant of the heart and brain., but at the same time it constricts blood vessels. Chronic use can lead to physical exhaustion, poor concentration, psychosis and sexual dysfunction. It increases the risk of heart attack heart failure, seizure and stroke. Alcohol is especially harmful to growing bodies. Drinking too much can cause dizziness, poor coordination, confusion, vomiting, unconsciousness, depression and liver disease. When a person drinks a lot of alcohol in a short time it can cause death. Thousands of babies are born with mental and physical defects because their teen mothers drank or smoked when they were pregnant. Alcohol abuse can lead to cancer, cirrhosis, brain damage, malnutrition and death.

Saul Rosen, PhD, M.D encourages people to make informed decisions on the use of drugs. Marijuana and LSD alter the perception of reality. They distort the way the senses work including the sense of time, space and self. Marijuana affects vision and hearing, Prolonged use of marijuana can cause coughing, wheezing, and pneumonia and lung just like cigarettes do. LSD can precipitate a psychotic episode; Paranoia, irresponsible behavior and lung disease have resulted from the use of marijuana. It affects the receptor cells that control muscle movement and memory storage. This explains why users often have loss of short-term memory. Scientific studies have shown that chronic administration can damage the brain's hippocampus and cause permanent memory impairment.

Alternative Activities to Balance Your Emotions

Here is a much safer process than taking the risk of mind-altering drugs which have life threatening side-effects. Establish a center of peace with focused thought, relaxation and self-care to set boundaries. Focus on the emotions of gratitude and compassion. Recognize invading emotions of fear, anger, depression and guilt. Exchange the feelings of hopelessness, indifference, doubt and self-pity for joy, peace and unconditional love. Act rather than react as you practice new habit patterns. Breath is the vehicle to bridge between the brain wave frequencies and dimensional realities. The following builds traits of self-awareness, self-confidence, maturity, responsibility and follow through.

Use breathing techniques, imagery, NLP and self-hypnosis to regulate emotions and gain a greater control of the mind and body. The more these are used, the more effective they become. Play calm music softly in the background for these imageries. Sit in a comfortable position with your spine erect and your eyes closed. Use the deepening breath technique by inhaling through the nose to the count of five and exhaling through the mouth to the count of five. Repeat five times and continue gentle relaxed breathing.

Pick any one of these suggested imageries and practice daily for five to ten minutes and come back to alert consciousness with the count of five:

As you inhale through the nose, imagine a stream of green light filling you with positive healing energy. Exhale through the mouth letting go of all negativity.

Imagine you are going down a staircase slowly one step at a time as you count backwards from ten to one. Be aware that your body is relaxing with each count. When you get to level one you are in your Heart Brain center where the emotions are stored and regulated. Gently draw in positive feelings on the inhale and release negative feelings on the exhale.

Imagine you are hitting a ball of golden energy far into the distance. Hit three of these energy balls, one following the other and each one goes much farther away than the last. The balls clear the way for positive thoughts, feelings and actions in the upcoming distance you will travel.

You are simply the observer and are watching from the safe protected place of a rainbow-colored bubble. Imagine a spinning large wheel in front of you, When this spins backward counterclockwise, it takes you back to reconstruct any past unhappiness using the process of NLP and self-hypnosis. Over lay positive events as you breathe in their reality. When it spins clockwise to the right, it goes forward in time to put in place desired future outcomes using the focus of your breath.

Imagine a beautiful sunset or sunrise. Absorb the colors of peach, lavender and blue.

Life Improvement by Redirecting Anger and Fear

Fear is at the base of anger. Fear of being out of control. You can correct this by realizing you have free will and are in control of your choices. You can't control another person, but you can control yourself and your reaction to your environment. You can change your environment. Anger affects the body in very destructive ways. It ages all organs, but the main harm goes to the liver. Note how you feel when you allow anger to take your over. Becoming aware of your feelings and emotions is the first step to regulating and controlling them. How do you feel when you let fear run your life and hold the crisis mode reality of fight or flight? Describe the stress that results and the effects it has on your body and mind and level of happiness. One thing leads to another as fear and anger escalate.

Establishing Your Center

If you need to prove something, you'll always have something to prove. People have wasted their entire life in this useless endeavor. Instead know your own worth so you won't be compelled by the need from others. Approval and agreement is simply given from others or it isn't no matter how hard you try to justify yourself. People will either be for you and excuse you, or they will be against you and blame you no matter what has happened. Don't go off on side roads to meet someone else's expectations. Live your life in a way you can be proud of yourself. You always have to face yourself so don't make yourself have to play games to tolerate who you are. The concepts you hold form the core of your approach to life.

* Let go of erroneous concepts such as these:
* I'm right. You are wrong. My worth depends on this.
* Life is unfair. I am a victim of what others decide to do for me. I am their emotional prisoner.
* It is my job to fix you. I will use all my life force to work on this goal rather than fixing myself.
* I care more about you than I do about me. I will spend most of my time in conflict with you.
* Replace these self-destructive concepts with the following affirmations:
* I can and do take care of myself first. Then I fill with love and can give for this reservoir within.
* "No" is a complete sentence that I assertively say and mean. I am in control of my responses.

The Power of Positive Thinking: Recognizing Destructive Patterns:

Each person tends to relate to his/her environment based on the early programming. of self-love. Do you give positive messages to yourself or putdowns? Is the glass half full or half empty? The way a person relates to others is based on either a positive or negative relationship they have with themselves. A good starting point to evaluate how you are relating to yourself is observe your response to these questions:

1. Do you like who you are? Are you a victim or a go-getter?

2. Are you a problem-oriented or solution-oriented person? Were your parents this way? Have you just assumed their approach to life or do you have your own?

3. Do you look for the lessons in the challenges that your life experience offers.

4. Are you ready to have a simple, easy flowing life? What will it take to accomplish this?

Studies indicate a person tends to bring about what they believe. The expectation becomes the reality. Thin Big and affirm this or something better. Imagine what you want rather than what you fear. The mind works like a computer and holds the neurological loops of thoughts and reactions in your mind. New habits are formed by imaging patterns of twenty-one repetitions.

Positive Thinking Assignment

Affirm to say only positive things for twenty-one days. Journal your reactions. Many changes can be implemented when you say only uplifting things to and about other people and situations. Look for the good in everything. What an adventure! How well do you know yourself? Take a stand in life by deciding what your stand for. How much will you stand in your life? Does it support your growth? What do you respect in yourself? List your hot buttons. List your stereotypes and prejudices.

Having Fun/ Having Respect

Having fun is based on your attitude. You can find pleasure in the simplest activity. Some people can spend large amounts of money and still be bored or unhappy. Others find joy because they live in a state of gratitude and anticipation. Begin to look for the things others don't even see. Most anything can be fun by the way you feel about it whether you are alone of sharing it with someone else. Here are a few suggestions to increase the joy in life:

Take a walk noticing the beauty in nature, appreciating the colors, smells and animals.

Watch a child at play.

Fill your heart with love and be grateful.

Three Codes of Conduct to Live By

Honor Yourself

Do I only do those things for which I am proud? Do I act with integrity? Do I play games? Am I a victim of someone else's games? Do I honor my time? Do I protect my inner child? Do I honor myself by setting reasonable boundaries?

Honor Your Words

Do what you say you will do. If you break your word, other lose trust I you. Be where you told others you will be or call and explain the delay.

Honor Others

Answer politely in a respectful tone of voice. Avoid all these behaviors by and to you: ignoring the other person, keeping them waiting, walking off without speaking, giving a dirty look, snapping in a hateful or condescending tone.

Me and My Parents

Many parents live vicariously through their child. Are you living your life to fulfil your own goals or theirs? Is this your life or theirs?

Give your response to these relationships: Mother, Father, Child

- — Do I have a healthy bond with my parents?
- — Express the ways you are alike and different that your father.
- — Express the ways you are alike and different that your mother.
- — Am I at peace with my parents? If not, what do I need to do to resolve this?
- — Can I be me and still feel accepted and loved by my parents?

Free to Be Me

A person can lose oneself in a relationship. Taking care of yourself means defining your own thoughts and feeling. To clarify your own identity, ask yourself these questions:

- — What are my expectations for my life? Are these mine or other people's?
- — What games do I allow myself to play? Are these mine or other peoples'?
- — What needs do I allow to run my life? Are these mine or other people's?
- — Am I living the goals for my life dream or someone else's?
- — What anger do I allow to consume me? Is this anger mine or does it belong to someone else?
- — What fear do I allow to own me? Are these min or other people's?
- — Do I place my happiness in the hands of other people? Name whose hands!
- — Do I lose myself in codependency? Am I an enabler?
- — What are the values I hold? Are these mine or other peoples'?

— Do I live in fantasy dream or in realty?
— How can I make a more fulfilling life for myself without being codependent on others?
— Do pestlets run my life? Are these coming from me or from other people?
— Do I live with grievances and regrets? Have I forgiven myself and other people?
— Do I accept other people's opinion of me as valid without personal introspection?

Building Boundaries and Bridges

What are my personal boundaries? Establish your limits. This is a point of contact physically, verbally and emotionally that another person will not be allowed to go beyond. Did these patterns start in my childhood, or later in school to be accepted and to feel love?

Here are examples of boundaries that need to be set:

- o Hitting, violence (physical abuse)
- o Nagging (emotional abuse)
- o Promises which are not kept (emotional abuse)
- o Yelling (emotional abuse)
- o Criticism, blame and shame (emotional abuse)
- o Guilt and self-blame (self-abuse)
- o Do I cross boundaries with other people in my relationships or let others walk over mine?
- o Do I use these: Assertive voice tone, eye contact, conviction, determination, follow through

Why doesn't a person set boundaries? Do these behaviors describe you?

- o Self-doubt and insecurity (Not good enough to replace what we risk losing by having limits.
- o Fear of being alone
- o Fear of being hurt physically if you speak up for yourself
- o Self-invalidation
- o Martyr
- o Guilt
- o Self-denial (Distorted view of reality that things are not as bad as the really are.)
- o Desensitized from long term abuse
- o Mixed feelings

Self-introspection of Verbal Conduct

- o Do I issue orders?
- o Am I loud and boisterous?
- o Do people seem to pull away from me?
- o Am I overbearing?
- o Am I pushy?
- o Am I truly concerned about other?
- o Am I offensive?
- o Am I intimidating?
- o Am I a bully?

Three Rules for Getting Better Responses

  ✱ Be empathetic
  ✱ Be gentle
  ✱ Be calm

Effective Conflict Resolution Skills

  ○ Do I speak directly about my own feelings and needs? Am I heard?
  ○ Do I avoid telling other people how I felt in a conflict?
  ○ Do I use a calm voice in controversial discussions?
  ○ Do I understand the other person's point of view?
  ○ Do I make the other person feel heard and understood?
  ○ Is winning more important than getting both our needs meet?
  ○ Can I let go of the battle to resolve the power struggle?
  ○ Do I negotiate a compromise in disputes with another person?
  ○ Do I feel compromise is losing?
  ○ Is it right for one person to give up all they originally wanted in an encounter?
  ○ Can I take a deep breath and calm down during a conflict?
  ○ Can I look at the other person's side of a conflict to work out a solution?
  ○ Do I respond or react?

Re-Sourcing and Re-Structuring

This process is designed to aid mindful action and to synchronize your emotions free of all past and future attachments. By re-sourcing one can harmonize higher energy fields into your mind and body. Participants can use this cumulative effect of "Life Restructuring" to assist the inner journey of self-discovery.

Controlling one's self is directly related to power issues and self-love. A decision must be based on self-worth if one is going to be controlled from within or from without. It is necessary for the teen to have an internal value code of what he/she believes and what they will sacrifice to get basic needs fulfilled. These value systems will either come from the heritage and the home or form the peers and pop culture norms.

Ultimately it is up to each individual to be one's own guidance system and to protect what is valued. Positive interactions will only be possible when control issues are not confused with efforts to manipulate the environment. Respect is the key. Know who you are and allow others to be who they are.

The Virtues Project was founded in the early 1990's to provide empowerment strategies for families and professional development programs to create a culture of character in homes schools, prisons and corporations. The goal is to have mentorship for teens from parents, community and police that model integrity. This sponsors five strategies based on virtues of greater joy, justice and unity including:

Speak the Language: The power of words discourages or inspires. The Virtues Language helps replace shaming and blaming with personal responsibility and respect. It is a frame of reference for bringing out the best in children and adults. It helps us all become the kind of people we want to be.

Recognizing Teachable moments: When we have the humility and self-confidence to learn from our mistakes, every stumbling block becomes a steppingstone.

Set Clear Boundaries: Virtues-based boundaries are focused on respect, restoration of justice and reparation to create a climate of peace and safety. Personal boundaries help build healthy relationships which protect our time and our energy.

Honor the Spirit: This means respecting the dignity of each person. This strategy encourages us to make time for reflection, and beauty to participate in the arts. Honoring special life events in our stories helps connect to our heritage and values.

Self-Image and Success

Some people never stop and think about the following. Have You?

- What are my opinions about myself in these areas?
- My hair
- My weight
- My personality
- My self-discipline
- My emotional balance
- My organizational ability
- My use of time
- My control of money
- What do I think others think of me? Does this bother, uplift or matter to me?
- Do I make my own choices and think for myself or go with the crowd?
- Can I make a goal plan and stick to it?
- What three things do I want most in life?
- How do I plan to get them?
- When will I get started on the process of this plan?
- Where will I be in this process one year from now?
- Where will I be in this process three years from now?

In her book "The Family Virtues Guide," Linda Kavelin Popov gives a process to introduce this to your family. Show them the following Virtues List. Each person will choose a virtue from the Gifts of Character that he/she wants to work on in themselves and then share their experiences in a week in a Sharing Circle. Every person involved is to choose their own virtue, not suggest one someone else needs to work on.

The Gifts of Character in the Virtues Project

Assertiveness, Caring, Cleanliness, Commitment, Compassion, Confidence, Consideration, Courage, Courtesy, Creativity, Detachment, Determination, Diligence, Enthusiasm Excellence, Flexibility, Forgiveness, Friendliness, Generosity, Gentleness, Helpfulness, Honesty, Honor, Humility, Idealism,

Integrity, Joyfulness, Justice, Kindness, Love Loyalty, Moderation, Modesty, Orderliness Patience, Peacefulness, Perseverance, Purposefulness, Reliability, Respect, Responsibility, Self-discipline, Service, Tact, Thankfulness, Tolerance, Trust, Trustworthiness, Truthfulness, Understanding, Unity

Being at Peace with Oneself

In her book "The Business of Kindness," by Oliva McIvers states, "If you want to live in a world of kindness and compassion, you must walk the talk. It must be created in your inner being and outward acts."

If you are to live a life of tranquility, peace and joy, you need to make a plan to do live these qualities in the following areas of your relationships:

Kindness to oneself – authenticity, attitude, resilience, excellence

Kindness to one's school associates- trust, compassion, courage, friendship

Kindness in the community – service, responsibility, integrity, tolerance

The Importance of Attitude

We must control our response to external events, actions and opinions of others to build resilience in these changing times. Our attitude will spread to all our professional and personal relationships for better or worse.

One's attitude is the perception which determines the way you respond to a stimulus. Foster a proactive approach by creating a healthy and vibrant lifestyle as you examine your own behavior and thoughts. Each person's reality is based on their attitude about what has happened. A healthy goal is to focus on positives to diminish stress if you are to find excellence and meaning in your work and lift your family and friends.

McIvor writes, "Speak your truth with honesty and integrity by demonstrating you are as good as your word." When you only say something and don't follow through, it breaks not only peace between you and others, it breaks trust. If people can't trust you to do what you say, they will come to feel you are not reliable. When trust goes, everything goes downhill. Being able to trust someone depends on feeling they care about your needs and are doing what is in your best interest. Speaking truth empowers a person.

Compassion is directly related to the ability to speak in ways that can be heard. It is about motivating others to their best potential. If you stand true to your word, it is one way to live leadership principals. By providing a safe supportive environment full of goodwill and respect, you can build character to have the courage to make changes and do what is right even in the face of personal adversity.

When a person acts with compassion and the kindness of their sacred word given in friendship, we can do anything more effectively. Gratitude is also a genuine act of friendship. The dictionary defines compassion as "a deep awareness of and sympathy for another's suffering. It is the humane quality of understanding the suffering of others and wanting to do something about it." An anonymous quote relates "We are here to walk each other home." McIvor challenges, "Is there someone in your life or at workplace who needs someone to walk them home?"

When you pay attention to the little things, you give those around you the gift of witnessing your gratitude for people's presence in your life. When you pay kindness forward out of friendship, you are sharing the ability for other to show gratitude. Each of us is encouraged to do ten acts of random kindness and then write how it affects you. This can have an important benefit to change. Let Kindness Sprinklet lead your behavior.

Kindness in the community involves continual altruistic service and a true concern for the welfare of others and our planetary resources. We are each called to commit to our responsibility to lead positive change more actively. This involves doing the right thing to bring justice, fairness, equality and sustainability. You are challenged to see if your words motivate, inspire and support or do they reject, humiliate and condemn.

Being tolerant comes when you move from the norm of common ground to higher ground by being able to apologize. All people must come to the place of tolerance and strength in diversity. Kindness starts with a state of mind. It is the time to live as a global family and build community. We must accept one person can make a difference and ask, "What am I doing for others?"

Active Listening

Active listening takes being totally present, open and responsive to the words and ideas of another person. Listening is an effective peace building skill. This is accomplished by focusing your attention on what the other person is trying to relate and incorporate active listening. Sometimes all a person needs to make their life turn a corner is to be heard. When someone gives you their attention, it is a compliment. We need to be respectful, listen and not try to fix them in any way or feel it is our responsibility to teach them something. This is disrespectful and condescending to think we have an answer for them when they haven't ask for our opinion. In order to establish more peaceful communication, we can make an effort to reach out and be more encouraging to those with whom we come in contact.

Peaceful Affirmations for Teens

* I am committed to authentically be distinctly myself.
* I will use my choices to be distinct instead of dissolving into the mainstream.
* I am committed to be authentic by cultivating awareness of what is most important to me. I allow others to see my true self.
* I live in the moment authentically and joyfully.
* My words are honest and are delivered in a kind way.
* I live the values I believe in.
* I continuously challenge myself to go beyond my personal comfort zone.
* I am living my values and follow through to bring my goals into being.
* I am changing my vocabulary to be more powerful every day in everyway
* I am enhancing my inner control and support my vocabulary with the words "I choose" instead of saying "I have to" or "I should."
* I accept responsibility for my life and see the perfection of my life lessons.
* I count my blessings and am responsible for the quality of my own life.
* I am pleased and enlivened with the benefit I gain from my thoughts and feelings.
* I respect my feelings and those of others.
* I use time engaging in activities and conversations that are uplifting.
* I continue to inspire meaning and help others find a sense of purpose in their work.
* I celebrate who I am and what I have accomplished this very day and every day.
* I am focused on positive thoughts of the present and let go of the experiences of the past.
* I nurture my body, mind and spirit by being in nature each day and exercising regularly.
* I recommit to all my personal goals to take charge of my life.
* *Create five more positive affirmations of your own*

Current Goal Journal

List the qualities that you are choosing to let go.

Write down six things you are grateful for.

In order to grow the peace-building trait of *responsibility*, I can support a healthier and kinder environment if I do the following:

* ✱ Name two habits you would like to eliminate.
* ✱ Reflect on these questions regarding the peace building trait of *Tolerance*:
* ✱ Do you have a tendency to contribute or condemn?
* ✱ How do you feel if you have built walls of judgment?
* ✱ List areas you need to consider becoming more tolerant of others.

I can support a kinder environment if I do the following:

* ✱ I refuse to say anything that is not uplifting to a situation or the people involved.
* ✱ I am more tolerant of my own actions and past learning lessons.
* ✱ I continue to affirm that all people are precious and treat them accordingly.
* ✱ I am committed to be authentic by cultivating awareness of what is most important to me.
* ✱ I allow others to see my true self.
* ✱ I live in the moment authentically and joyfully.
* ✱ My words are honest and are delivered in a kind way.
* ✱ I live the values I believe in.

Resolving Differences

When two people argue, it means they are looking at two different perspectives of a situation. Resolving their differences can be accomplished if both parties are willing. If both people focus on being honest about their own actions and feelings, the level of conflict diminishes. This requires a specific peace-building process that involves setting the priority of listening to one another and talking rather than bickering with angry words aimed at winning. If the goal is to 'win' or to protect one's ego, everyone will lose. Protecting the self-worth of both people and allowing both to be heard is the key to resolution.

When time is lost fighting, it can never be recouped. Painful words are not forgotten, and it becomes harder and harder to accomplish a peaceful relationship. Eventually game playing makes this impossible. The following are some of the basic techniques used in playing games to win. Note the suggested beneficial behavior is written in italics after each game playing behavior to incorporate constructive resolution.

Diversion: If either one approaches communication by the use of diverting tactics to change the subject, the frustration level is raised by the other person who is trying to get to the point of the issue at hand. Arguments are accelerated over bringing in other issues. Keep on track with the issue that is up for discussion.

Ego Issues: If the ego won't let the person be honest with themselves about mistakes or limitations, then phony excuses raise the level of conflict. Humility comes from true inner security and allows a person to be honest with themselves and others about any short comings. Be secure enough to be honest.

Loaded Questions: Asking a question to lead the other person into a trap involves asking something you clearly know the answer to and interrupting before they can finish answering. When a question is asked, let the other person answer. Listen with the intention of really hearing what he/she is saying.

Lack of Attention: If the purpose of the discussion is to make it a debate, each person will be so busy thinking of their next response, there is a lack of attention to what the other person is really saying. Listen with the purpose of compromise which is a 'win-win' situation.

Looking Within at Your Own Behavior

Focus of Focus: If the argument leads to issues of fault and blame, the tendency is to focus on the other person, rather than take responsibility for one's own part in what is now becoming an escalating crisis. If person number one starts pointing a finger and telling person number two how number two is feeling, nothing worthwhile is accomplished.

Denial: Refusing to acknowledge one's anger level and feelings is the primary reason that a disagreement turns into a heated argument. Acting with integrity incorporates looking within at the character traits you are demonstrating in every situation to bring self-awareness and inner control over you own behavior.

Assumptions: This is when instead of talking the issue out, one or both persons, decide what the other is thinking. Since this is usually based on where the person making the assumption is coming from, it is usually wrong. Being alert to the present moment is the key to realizing the other person may have changed his/her mind or is ready to let it go.

Silent Treatment: Clamming up is actually abandonment. Avoiding the other person by going into another room or leaving the house is avoidance and makes thigs worse. If both parties could agree to spend ten or fifteen minutes remembering the priority of their love and work on calming down, then they could at least start the reconciliation process. 'Silence is golden' when it is used to start thinking of ways to heal the discord. Being ready to reconcile avoids losing precious time that could be spent enjoying time together.

Avoidance: Stuffing the disagreement is a refusal to deal with clarifying and validating everyone who is involved. The 'forgiveness and make up stage' of a disagreement turns into an unresolved fight that festers and builds walls. Building bridges is a wiser activity. **Intimidation:** Speaking in a tone that is meant to put the other person on the defensive only builds discord and distance. This involves the process of 'taking no prisoners.' It is simply about crushing the opponent and destroys the foundation of any friendship. This dirty tactic will never be a part of any productive interactions. If the two people remember that they agreed to be on the same team, safety can be established.

Interrogation: Drilling questions in a hostile manner is only meant to gain an edge in what has become a fight and has nothing to do with really getting answers. It is more like hurling words as weapons to wound. Using sprinklet words that heal, and bond is the best way to maintain peaceful communication.

Eight Week Self-Improvement Program

This is an Eight Week Self-Improvement Program to guide introspection of your communication skills with yourself and with others. The goal is to enhance your quality of life.

Honesty is the quality to focus on for week one.

Watch your emotions as though you are in the audience watching a movie of your feelings and resulting behavior. The first step in change is awareness of the truth and acknowledgement of things as they are. Realize we have all done the best we could in any situation based on our awareness at the time. Foster the ability to feel and express the entire range of human emotions. The goal is to learn ways to take personal responsibility for your own actions/reactions and to control them, rather than being controlled by them.

Compassion is the focus for week two.

Make a list of your best qualities and a list of the qualities you admire in your loved ones. Write these two lists in the form of affirmations as in these examples: I am funny. I am easy going. My friends are kindhearted. The goal is to establish a positive foundation in your core concept of self and others. We are being considerate role models.

Vigilance is the focus for week three.

Draw a circle and list all your best qualities inside this circle. When you find yourself outside the circular boundary of your *better self*, pull your focus back into your higher qualities. Be vigilant so that other emotions do not take over and cause you to express yourself in a hurtful manner. The goal is to stop negative thoughts, attitudes and influences whether they come from inside of you or outside in your environment.

Gratitude is the focus for week four.

Count your blessings. Look for the good in all people and in all situations. The goal is to have a grateful attitude, seek the lesson in your encounters, then move forward to better interactions.

Mindfulness is the focus for week five.

Be mindful of what is happening at the moment and be totally present. Put your full attention on what you are doing so your thoughts will not be wandering to other things. Become aware of everything you see, feel, smell and touch. Increase your sensitivity to your enjoyment of these sensory experiences. The goal is to enhance all your senses and to listen more effectively.

Kindness is the focus for week six.

Concentrate on saying things in kinder voice tones. The goal is to be uplifting in your communication skills and express respect for yourself and others with your words.

Flexibility is the focus for week seven.

Allow change because it is necessary for growth and progress to take place. Be open-minded to recognize any stubbornness, stereotyping and outgrown thought patterns. The goal is to accept a more efficient way of conducting your life activities.

Goal Setting is the focus for week eight.

Focus on the ideal situation you would like to attain in your life in three areas including personal growth, social relations and career or attainment goals. Establish a Self-improvement Plan consisting of nine goals. Set a short-term goal in each of these three areas of your life to accomplish in one month. These are to be a part of a longer-term self-improvement plan. Set another goal in each of the three life areas to accomplish in six months. Finally set another goal in each of the three life areas to accomplish in three years. Take action to work your goal plan day by day and be patient with your progress.

IFGP (Individual Family Goal Plan)

Answer the following self-awareness questionnaire with A, B, or C.

A. This is very true of me.

B. This is somewhat true of me.

C. This is not at all true of me.

_____ I make my own choices and am responsible for the results of these.

_____ I am self-confident.

_____ I forgive myself easily.

_____ I forgive others easily.

_____ I need to be right.

_____ I am organized.

_____ I feel a sense of accomplishment and productivity when I finish a task.

_____ I am a self-starter.

_____ I am in control or my actions.

_____ I have firm boundaries.

_____ I do things with my time that are beneficial to me.

_____ I set goals and accomplish them on time.

_____ I know what I want in my relationships.

My interests are _____

My talents are _____

My goals are_____

Motivation

If an individual doesn't have a destination, it is harder to get started. Set a goal! Get a plan! Don't just be a dreamer. Be a dreamer who makes you heart felt dreams become a reality. Be a person who inspires others to their highest potential by your belief in them. An action oriented, goal directed person can motivate others by simply being on their path of forward motion. A couch potato isn't going to get anyone going. Don't let this be you.

<u>Stick to Your Principles</u>

An individual can make a difference,

Each time a person stands up for an ideal

A tiny ripple of hope is sent out.

Eventually the whole world is affected.

Learn to choose healthy role models.

May the Stars guide your ways and fill your days with Sprinklets.

About the Author

Patrice Joy, MA is a licensed interfaith minister and has over forty years of experience in the field of education, business, family dynamics and Integrative Health. Her educational degrees from Antioch McGregor University are a Bachelor of Arts with a double major in Health and Wellness and Human Development and a Master of Arts in Community Change and Civic Leadership. As a Reiki Master Instructor and Herbal Master, she utilizes several forms of vibrational medicine. Patrice has taught at Webster University and Forest Park Community College. She was the first woman hired in territorial sales management for the Xerox Corporation and was hostess of the TV Series entitled *The Parent's Role.* Patrice presented programs for several government agencies including CASA, Head Start, Salvation Army, Fresh Start and One Stop and presented workshops for USAF Falcon Trail Youth Camp, USAFA Family Advocacy and Older Moms Coalition. She was voted Woman of the Year in the Women's Professional Organization in 2011/2012. Her leadership skills have led her to the founding of Creative Learning Programs, Western Celebrations, Seekers of Serenity (SOS) Nonprofit and Harmonizing Health Wisdom.

About the Illustrator

Kristen Croxton graduated from Hanover College with a BA in Studio Art. She earned the Greiner Award for her senior project entitled Possible Possibilities. This innovative work remains on permanent display. Kristen wants to motivate people to realize the power of art in the healing process and to inspire people to reach their highest potential. Her main life lesson has been to follow her heart and her life path has culminated in a unique blend of Christian Spirituality that honors the teachings of Jesus. She enjoys the psychological aspect of the Sprinklet and Pestlet Series that depicts positive moral values.

Patrice can be contacted at healingfeelings333@gmail.com

More information is available at *harmonizinghealthwisdom*

Bibliography

Amen, Daniel. G. M.D. (2008) *Magnificent Mind At Any Age*, NY, Harmony Books

Andrews, T. (1993). *The Healer's Manual.* St. Paul, MN: Llewwllyn Press.

Begley, S. (2007). *Train Your Mind Change Your Life*. New York, NY: Ballatine Books.

Benson, H. (1976). *The Relaxation Response.* New York, NY: Avon Books.

Bruch, H. M.D. (1979). *The Golden Cage*. Cambridge, MA: University Press.

Byron L. & Pucelik, F., (1990). *NLP Demystified*. Portland, OR: Metamorphose Press.

Caprio, F. M.D. & Berger, J. (1998). *Healing Yourself with Self Hypnosis*. New York, NY: Prentice Hall Press.

Carper, J. (2000). *Your Miracle Brain.* New York, NY: Harper Collins Press.

Childre, Doc, & Martin, Howard, Beech, Donna (1999) *The Heartmath Solution*, San Francisco, Ca, HarperCollins, Publishing

Childre, Doc & Rozman, Deborah, PhD, (2005), Oakland, CA, New Harper Publication Inc.

Cousins, N. (1979). *Anatomy of an Illness*. New York, NY: Bantam Book & W. Norton.

Crick, F. (1994). *The Astonishing Hypotheses: The Scientific Search for the Soul*. New York, NY: Simon & Schuster

Davidson, Richard, PhD. (2013) *The Emotional Life of Your Brain,* London, England, Penguin Books

Davis, L. (1990). *The Courage to Heal Workbook.* New York, NY: Harper Collins.

DeBono, E. (1994). *De Bono Thinking Course*. New York, NY: Facts on File Inc.

Dudley, G. (1975). *Increase Your Learning Power.* Hollywood, CA: Wilshire Books.

Freedom, John, (2013) *Emotional Freedom Technique,* London, NWI, Hodder & Stoughton

Gendlin, E., PhD, (2007). *Focusing.* New York, NY: Bantam Books.

Goleman, D. (1994). *Emotional Intelligence.* New York, NY: Random House Press.

Goleman, T. (2001). *Emotional Alchemy*. New York, NY: Three Rivers Press.

Grundy, Steven R., MD, *(2019) The Plant Paradox,* Broadway, NY, HarpersCollins Pub.

Hart. A. (1995). *Adrenaline and Stress.* Wheaton, IL: Tydale House Publications.

Hay, L. (1994). *You Can Heal Your Life*. Carson, CA: Hay House Inc.

Harris, T. (1955). *I'm OK, You're OK*. New York, NY: Harpers and Row Publishers.

Hersch, Patricia (19980. *A Tribe Apart*. Westminster, London: Penguin Press Books

Hicks, J. (2007). *The Astonishing Power of Emotions*. Carlsbad, CA: Hay House Inc.

Howard, P. (2000). *The Owner's Manual for The Brain*. 2nd Ed. Austin, TX: Bard Press.

Kabat-Zinn, J. (2005). *Coming To Our Senses*. New York, NY: Hyperion Press.

Knaster, M. (1996). *Discovering The Body's Wisdom*. New York, NY: Bantam Books.

Langer, E. (1997). *The Power of Mindful Learning*. Cambridge, MA: DaCapo Press.

Lawlis, F. M.D. (2006). *The IQ Answer*. New York, NY: Penguin Group Press.

Lawlis, F. M.D. (2008). *The Stress Answer*. New York, NY: Penguin Group Press.

Lewis, B. & Pucelik, F. (1990). *Magic NLP Demystified*. Portland, OR: Metamorphous.

Lipton, B. (2004). *The Biology of Belief*. Santa Rosa, CA: Elite Books.

Mahony, T. (2007). *Making Your Words Work: Using NLP to Improve Communication, Learning & Behavior*. Carmarthen, Wales England: Crown House Publishing.

Maloney, M.D. & Kranz, R. (1991). *Straight Talk About Eating Disorders*. New York, NY: Bantam Double Day Publishing.

Maltz, M., (1960). *Psychocybernetics*. New York, NY: Prentice Hall Inc.

Maltz, M., (1993). *Psychocybernetics 2000*. Paramus, NJ: Prentice Hall Inc.

McCarthy, J. & Kartzinel, J. (2009). *Healing and Preventing Autism*. New York, NY: Penguin Press.

Minchinton, J. (1993). *Maximum Self-Esteem*. Vanzant, MO: Arnford House Publishers.

Murphy, J. (2000). *Power of Your Sub-conscious Mind*. New York, NY: Bantam Books.

Myss, C. & Shealy, N. (1993). *Creation of Health*. New York, NY: Three Rivers Press.

Ornish, D. (2007). *The Spectrum*. New York, NY: Ballantine Books.

Patel, M., (1993). *Your Personal Peace Formula*. Wiltshire, England: Life Foundation Publications.

Pink, D. (2006). *A Whole New Mind*. New York NY: Riverhead Books.

Rubin, J. (2003). *Patient, Heal Thyself*. Topanga, CA: Freedom Press.

Sandstrom, K., Martin, D. Fine, G.. (2006). *Symbols, Selves, and Social Reality*. New York, NY: Oxford University Press.

Silva, J. (1977). *The Silva Mind Control Method*. New York, NY: Pocket Books.

Silva J. & Stone R. (1989). *You, The Healer*. Tiburon, CA: H.J. Kramer Inc.

Smith, L. (1976). *Improving Your Child's Behavior Chemistry*. Englewood, Cliffs, NJ: Prentice-Hall Publishing.

Sternberg, E. (2001). *The Balance Within: The Science Connecting Health and Emotions*. New York, NY: W.H. Freeman & Company Publishing.

Truman, K. (1991). *Feelings Buried Alive Never Die*. Las Vegas, NV: Olympus Press.

Weil, A. (1995). *Spontaneous Healing*. New York, NY: Alfred A. Knopf Inc.

Wehrenberg, M. (2008). *The 10 Best Anxiety Management Techniques*. New York, NY: W.W. Norton Press.

Wheatley, M. (2006). *Leadership and the New Science*. San Francisco, CA: Berrett-Koehler Publishers Inc.

Widdowson, Mark, (2010) Transactional Analysis, London and NY, Routledge Publication

www.ingramcontent.com/pod-product-compliance
Lightning Source LLC
Chambersburg PA
CDIIW081153090426
42736CB00017B/3300